The Looking-glass

THE

LOOKING-GLASS:

CONTAINING

SELECT FABLES OF
LA FONTAINE,

IMITATED IN ENGLISH;

WITH

ADDITIONAL THOUGHTS.

VELUTI IN SPECULUM.

Interdum fpeciofa locis, morataque rectè
Fabula, nullius veneris, fine pondere et arte,
Valdius oblectat populum, meliufque moratur
Quam verfus inopes rerum, nugæque canoræ.
HOR. ART. POET.

LONDON:
PRINTED FOR J. WALTER, CHARING-CROSS.

M.DCC.LXXXIV.

ADVERTISEMENT.

THE Author of the following Imitations had never read Fontaine, till he very lately met with *Letters on feveral Subjects, by the Reverend Martin Sherlock, A. M. Chaplain to the Right Honourable the Earl of Briftol, in 2 vols. publifhed in* 1781. Mr. Sherlock is an Enthufiaft, and his panegyric upon Fontaine (which I fhall tranfcribe) perhaps hyperbolical. — Fontaine has neverthelefs been always confidered, by thofe who have ftudied the ftyle and manner of all Mythologifts, both ancient and modern, as an Author *fui generis.*

Select

Select Fables of Esop and other Fabu-
lists, in three books, in prose, were some time
since published by Mr. Dodsley : they were
written in a very elegant and ingenious
style.

In his judicious Essay on Fable, pre-
fixed to his Work, " the Author treats
" of the Moral—the Action—the Inci-
" dents—the Persons—the Characters—the
" Sentiments—and the Language of Fable :
" and in his Introduction to his Essay, ob-
" serves, that whoever composes a Fable,
" whether of the sublimer and more com-
" plex kind, as the Epic and Dramatic ;
" or of the lower and more simple kind,
" sometimes called Esopean ; must first
" endeavour to illustrate some one moral
" or prudential Maxim. It is the busi-
" ness of both to teach some particular
" Moral, exemplified by an Action, and
" this enlivened by moral Incidents.—I
                                        " would

" would by no means however infer (fays
" our Author) that to produce one of
" thefe fmall pieces, requires the fame
" degree of genius, as to form an *Epic* or
" *Dramatic Fable*. All I would infinuate
" is, that the Apologue has fome right to
" a fhare in our efteem, from the relation
" it bears to the Poems before mentioned;
" as it is honourable to fpring from 'a
" noble ftem, although in ever fo remote
" a branch. A perfect Fable, even of this
" inferior kind, feems a much ftronger
" proof of genius, than the mere narrative
" of an event: the latter, indeed, re-
" quires judgment; the former, together
" with judgment, demands an effort of the
" imagination.—Having thus endeavoured
" to procure thefe little compofitions as
" much regard as they may fairly claim,
" I proceed to treat of fome particulars
" more effential to their characters.

A 3   " Strictly

" Strictly fpeaking (continues our Au-
" thor) detached or explicit Morals are
" not neceffary : thofe we find at the clofe
" of Efop's Fables, were placed there by
" other hands. Among the Ancients,
" Phædrus, and Gay, among the Moderns,
" inferted theirs at the beginning. La
" Motte prefers them at the conclufion :
" and Fontaine difpofes of them indifcri-
" minately at the beginning or end." As
our Author proceeds, he treats of the Action and Incidents proper for a Fable :
—" Three conditions (he fays) are altoge-
" ther expedient : firft, it muft be clear—
" fecondly, it muft be one and entire—
" thirdly, it muft be natural."

In our Author's third fection, he treats
of the Perfons, Characters, and Sentiments
of the Fable,—and in the laft, of the Language.—" The Style of a Fable (he fays)
" muft be fimple and familiar, correct and
                              " elegant.

" elegant.—By the former, I would advise,
" that it should not be loaded with figure
" and metaphor; that the disposition of
" words be natural; the turn of the sen-
" tences easy; and their construction un-
" embarrassed: by elegance, I would ex-
" clude all coarse and provincial terms; all
" affected and puerile conceits; all obso-
" lete and pedantic phrases: to this I would
" adjoin, as the word, perhaps, implies,
" a certain finishing polish, which gives a
" grace and spirit to the whole, and which,
" though it may always have the appear-
" ance of nature, is almost ever the effect
" of art. But, notwithstanding all that has
" been said, there are some occasions on
" which it is allowable, and even expedi-
" ent, to change the style. The language
" of a Fable must rise or fall in conformity
" to the subject. A Lion, when intro-
" duced in his regal capacity, must hold

A 4   " discourse

" difcourfe in a ftrain fomewhat more ele-
" vated than a country Moufe: the Lionefs
" becomes his queen, and the Beafts of
" the foreft are called his fubjects: a me-
" thod which offers at once to the imagi-
" nation, both the Animal and the Perfon
" he is defigned to reprefent. Defcriptions
" at once concife and pertinent, add a
" grace to Fable; but are then moft hap-
" py when included in the action: an
" epithet well chofen, is often a defcrip-
" tion in itfelf; and is fo much the more
" agreeable, as it the lefs retards us in the
" purfuit of the cataftrophe.—I might en-
" large much farther upon the fubject;
" but fhall only hint, that little ftrokes of
" humour, when arifing naturally from the
" fubject; and incidental reflections, when
" kept in due fubordination to the prin-
" cipal, add a value to thefe compofitions.
" Thefe latter, however, fhould be em-
                                    " ployed

" ployed fparingly, and with great addrefs,
" be very few and very fhort; it is fcarcely
" enough that they *naturally fpring* out of the
" fubject; they fhould be fuch as to appear
" neceffary and effential parts of the Fable:
" and when thefe embellifhments, pleafing
" in themfelves, tend to illuftrate the main
" action, they then afford *that namelefs*
" *grace remarkable in Fontaine*, and which
" perfons of the beft difcernment will more
" eafily conceive than they can explain."

I have tranfcribed a confiderable part
of Mr. Dodfley's Effay, with an intent
to introduce thofe readers to Fontaine,
who have never ftudied him; an Author,
from whom I have received fuch infinite
delight, that I could not refrain from a
poor attempt of imitating (for it is impoffible literally to tranflate) fome of his
felect Fables, that thofe who cannot read
him in his own language, may form, perhaps,

haps, a feeble idea of the original.—The
Reader will meet with fome new thoughts,
I dare not fay fuch as Fontaine would
have given us, had he been an Englifh-
man. I intended to have imitated moft
of his Fables, upon a fuppofition it would
have been an undertaking fimilar to none
in our language; for though our excellent Gay is an Author whofe works will
never die—Fontaine was not his Proto-
type. A further progrefs in my fcheme
would have produced a work of magni-
tude, which probably would never have
been read. I therefore prefent the Public
with but a fpecimen: if, contrary to my
expectations, it fhould be approved of, I
fhall with pleafure proceed, and produce
a fecond cargo; particularly defigning to
imitate the Fables I fhall felect, in as great
a variety of metre, as circumftances will
admit of, confidering my puerile publica-
tion

tion as a trifling fubftitute for a ride in a wet morning : my Mufe, therefore, by varying her paces as much as poffible, may probably meet with a more general approbation. I fhall conclude this Advertifement with Mr. Sherlock's Three Letters, intending to make all the world as much an admirer of Fontaine, as he is of Lady Hervey.

Vol. I. Letter XX.

A number of the firft wits of Paris being affembled at the houfe of a famous Lady *Bel Efprit*, talked naturally enough of Literature. The elevation of Corneille, and the pathos of Racine, the purity of Boileau, and the depth of Moliere, were fupported by different advocates. At laft, fays one, Suppofe we were all this inftant to be carried to the Baftile, and doomed to pafs there

the

the remainder of our days ; fuppofe that we were fuffered to have each, any Author's works we chofe, but that we were never to be permitted to make a fecond choice; who is the Author each man would choofe, to chear the drearinefs of perpetual folitude ? Let no one fpeak; but let every man write the name of the Author he would prefer. They all wrote the fame name. It was that of La Fontaine. A greater compliment, I fuppofe, never was paid a Writer.

Had a fimilar queftion been put at London, among Englifh wits, I fancy Shakefpear would have been named : in modern Rome it would have been Ariofto: in ancient Rome, I believe, it would have been Horace.

La Fontaine appears to me to be the Corregio of poetry. The Graces conducted the pen of the one, as they did the pencil

of

of the other. They have both negligences and inaccuracies, which they feem not to have troubled themfelves about. La Fontaine wrote a fable: when he read it, fays he, There's a fyllable too much in that line; to correct it, I muft change a word; that word expreffes happily my meaning: if I lofe it, I lofe a beauty, and I gain a faultlefs but infipid line. One beauty compenfates fix faults: the fault and the beauty fhall both reft. My line hobbles; but that word fhall imprefs a fentiment on the heart, or prefent a picture to the imagination.

Corregio painted his Night. His object was the Virgin and Child. The canvafs was large; and, fays he, I muft fill it. What fhall I put in the top?—Why, fome Angels. So he has fcattered three or four fprawling figures in the top of the picture: thefe, I fuppofe, he painted in a

morning,

morning, and never meant they fhould be looked at. If the eye wanders to any other part of my canvafs, thought he, it will not fix there; it will foon come back to my Child and Virgin. I meant to put my force *there*, to fhew there the magic powers of my pencil, and I difregaid the fuffrage of any man who is capable of condemning me for weaknefs, where I did not mean to be ftrong. If I have a leg ill-difpofed, or a finger ill-drawn, it is becaufe I did not think the drawing of that finger, or the difpofition of that leg, of any importance. I fought effect. I ftrove to animate my cloth, to paint foul and grace, to charm the eye, to touch the heart, to enchant the imagination—Have I fucceeded?

There never were two more amiable artifts than thofe: there never were two artifts whofe works excited more agreeable

able fenfations, nor whofe productions appear to have coft them lefs. Eafe and *naturalnefs* (I mean naïveté) diftinguifh them equally. Other artifts force you to admire them : thefe you feel yourfelf inclined to love. You are fatisfied with knowing the works of other poets and painters ; but you wifh to have been acquainted with the perfons of Corregio and La Fontaine.—— *O fortunati ambo ! Si quid mea——*

As I have faid Corregio is the La Fontaine of painting, fo I think Albano is its Anacreon, Raphael its Virgil, and Rubens its Homer.

LETTER XXI.

MADAME de la Sabliere, a woman of condition in France, who fhared with Lewis the Fourteenth the honour of patronifing La Fontaine, ufed to call him her Fable-tree *(fon Fablier)* : fhe faid he

3   produced

produced fables fpontaneoufly, as an apple-tree does apples. That is very prettily faid; and the natural eafe which runs through all his works, proves that this faying is as fenfible as pretty.

The French, with great reafon, are proud of this writer. The only author who can expect his works to live, is he who communicates inftruction agreeably; who forms to himfelf a fyftem of never departing from ftrict truth, and of prefenting pictures, drawn only from nature, in an agreeable and pleafing point of view. This author is La Fontaine. He is an infinuating moralift, who, whilft he feems only to think of amufing his readers, fteals into their hearts the mildeft and moft amiable virtues. His fenfe is always juft; but he had the art to drefs Philofophy with fmiles, and to render that Goddefs truly engaging, who feems only formed to command.

command.—No mortal ever told a ftory better: gaiety and good fenfe, reafon and grace, are mixed in all his narrations: rapid, precife, and varied, he never afto- nifhes, but never fails to charm. Reading his fables, you are furprifed; for what you have read does not look like compofition, it appears to be the language of an agree- able companion, who converfes with eafe, with elegance, and fpirit.

To many a critic, fuch a writer will appear fuperficial. They do not feel the fuperiority of talent that is requifite to convey luminous truths, and deep reflec- tions, with almoft apparent careleffnefs. Becaufe Wifdom *generally* wears a frown, they do not conceive that ever fhe can be taught to fmile: and *that* which confti- tutes a writer's greateft merit, his being able to convey *interefting matter* in an *eafy* manner, appears to them a proof of his

a   inferiority.

inferiority. Enchanting La Fontaine ! my model and my guide, dread not such judges: it is thy greateſt glory, and will inſure thy everlaſting fame, that thou haſt been able to attract thy reader by an eaſy brilliancy, and engage him afterwards by ſolid reaſon and profound morality.

LETTER XXII.

La Fontaine was a ſingular character: his ſoul was as ſimple as his underſtanding was acute. On account of that ſimplicity, and of his being often abſent in company, which gave him frequently an appearance of ſillineſs, he was called by his contemporary wits, *Le bon Homme.*—You know this phraſe is generally uſed by the French, when they ſpeak of a good-natured man who has ſcarce common ſenſe. As Boileau, Moliere, and Racine, were one day walking together in the park at Verſailles, they

saw

faw La Fontaine perched up in a tree, where he was poffibly compofing a fable: Racine and Boileau began to laugh at him. "Don't laugh at him," fays Moliere, "the *bon homme* will go farther than any "of us." La Fontaine's hourly increafing fame, proves the fuperiority of Moliere's penetration.

The object of this inimitable fabulift was to be ufeful: to be ufeful, he knew he muft be agreeable: to be agreeable, he knew he muft have variety. He fully attained his ends. He has fo tiffued wit, fenfe, and fentiment, in his works, that he. muft pleafe every fpecies of readers. He has fo many ideas, that, read him ever fo often, he is always new. He has fo many remarks which come home to every man's bofom, that he is always interefting. Like Horace, he is read with more pleafure and profit, in proportion as men advance in

life.

life. But a circumftance peculiar only to himfelf is, that the fame fable which charms the formed philofopher, fhall delight the thoughtlefs fchool-boy, and the giddy coquet.

" *Deux Coqs vivoient en paix, un Poule*
  " *furvint,*
" *Et voilà la guerre allumée;*
" *Amour tu perdis Troye—*"

How fimple, how rapid that narration! how lively, how graceful, how unexpected the apoftrophe! and with what inconceivable addrefs has he introduced into his apoftrophe a moral reflection! See too, how he has given dignity to his reflection, by bringing in the deftruction of Troy! This is another of La Fontaine's fecrets, to make a grand idea arife out of what is feemingly a frivolous fituation. Here we

7   are

are thinking only of Two Cocks, and by a single stroke of his pen we are placed in a superior order of things, and have brought before us the Iliad, the Æneid, Agamemnon, Priam, Helen, and Achilles.

Do me the pleasure to read that Fable (*Les Deux Coqs*). You are lazy; you'll not read; otherwise I should recommend to you, *Les Animaux malades de la Peste*; *La Fille*; *Le Paysan du Danube*; *Le Chêne & le Roseau*; *Le Chat, la Belette, & le petit Lapin*. You are a good creature, but an indolent and dissipated one · do then indulge your indolence and me together, and abandon yourself a single evening to the luxury of your slippers, to read this child of Nature, and favourite of the Graces. One Fable I am determined you shall read, that is, provided you read me; for here it is, *Les Deux Pigeons*, &c.

CON-

(xxiii)

C O N T E N T S.

The

ERRATA.

Page 35, line 1, *for* our faults, *read* a fault.
Page 48, line 5, *for* reproach, *read* reprove.
Page 76, line 1, *for* mother, *read* dam.
Page 124, line 12, *for* who'll, *read* who will.

THE

THE TWO PIGEONS.

TWO Pigeons there were, and they lov'd one another,
 But yet, not contented at home,
Nor regarding the tender remonſtrance of t'other,
 The one was determin'd to roam.

And ſhall I, ſays his ſiſter, be left to complain:
 To where would you fly, let me aſk ?
In pity to me, for thy dangers are mine,
 Undertake not the perilous taſk :

Cold

Les Deux Pigeons.

DEUX Pigeons s'aimoient d'amour tendre:
 L'un d'eux s'ennuyant au logis,
Fut aſſez fou pour entreprendre
Un voyage en lointain pays.
L'autre lui dit: Qu'allez vous faire ?
Voulez-vous quitter votre frere ?

B

L'abſence

Cold winterly ſtorms are, we know, not remote,

 You'll repent of your courage too late;

Hark! this moment the raven's ſad ominous throat,

 Forebodes ſome poor flutterer's fate:

I ſhall have, in your abſence, ſuch horrible nights,

 And ſhall dream of ſuch terrible battles

With our fell feather'd tyrants, hawks, eagles, and kites—

 Hark! it rains——how the dreadful ſtorm rattles!

O! have you not here all your heart can deſire,

 A ſupper at night, and a neſt,

In which we from danger can ſafely retire,

 And together contentedly reſt?

         Though

L'abſence eſt le plus grand des maux:

Non pas pour vous, cruel. Au moins que les travaux,

 Les dangers, les ſoins du voyage,

 Changent un peu votre courage.

Encor ſi la ſaiſon s'avançoit davantage!

Attendez les Zephirs. Qui vous preſſe? Un Corbeau

Tout à-l'heure annonçoit malheur à quelque oiſeau.

Je ne ſongerai plus que rencontre funeſte,

Que Faucons, que Rézeaux. Hélas! dirai-je, il plût.

 Mon frere, a-t-il tout ce qu'il veut,

 Bon ſcupé [...] le reſte?

           Ce

Though ftruck, and difhearten'd a little at fiift,

By this friendly remonftrance affail'd,

Yet to fee the wide world our poor fugitive's thirft

And impatient defire, prevail'd :

My abfence lament not, fays he, for I mean

But to take a fhort voyage, and then,

Having feen, my dear fifter, what is to be feen,

I fhall certainly fly back again;

When return'd, the ftrange wonderful tales I'll unfold,

With what exquifite pleafure you'll hear !

Ev'ry fyllable fhall be fo faithfully told,

That you'd fwear you yourfelf had been there.

Both

Ce difcours ébranla le cœur

De notre imprudent voyageur

Mais le défir de voir & l'humeur inquiéte

L'emportèrent enfin. Il dit. Ne pleurez point;

Trois jours au plus rendront mon ame fatisfaite:

Je reviendrai dans peu conter de point en point

Mes aventures à mon frere.

Je le défennuirai. quiconque ne voit guère

N'a guère à dire auffi. Mon voyage dépeint

Vous fera d'un plaifir extrême.

Je dirai: J'étois-là, telle chofe m'avint :

Vous y croirez être vous-même.

A cet

Both fhedding, alas! the reciprocal tear,

 And both billing a tender adieu,

He at laft, * without moving his wings, through the air

 With the fwifteft celerity-flew.

Soon 'twas dark, whilft a gathering ftorm in the fky

 Prefented itfelf to his view;

In the plain but one poor fingle tree could he fpy,

 To which with impatience he flew ·

But its branches were few, and fo leaflefs with age,

 Little fhelter the wretch could obtain,

Whofe feathers were cruelly drench'd with the rage

 And the violent force of the rain.

When

* Celeres nec commovet alas. VIRGIL.

A ces mots, en pleurant, ils fe dirent adieu.

Le voyageur s'éloigne ; & voilà qu'un nuage

L'oblige de chercher retraite en quelque lieu :

Un feul arbre s'offrit, tel encor que l'orage

Maltraita le Pigeon, en dépit du feuillage.

L'air

When the ſtorm was blown over, and bright was the day,
 Having preened all his plumage anew,
By misfortune unluckily guided——away
 Once again the poor wanderer flew.

Soon, as if accidentally ſcatter'd, he ſpy'd,
 Poor fool! not accuſtom'd to faſt,
Some chaff, amidſt which a tame pigeon was ty'd,
 Which enjoy'd the pretended repaſt:

Eſcaping thoſe dangers which others beſet,
 To decoy ſhe was cunningly taught,
For the ſtranger, ſuſpecting no treacherous net,
 Soon deſcending, was ſuddenly caught:

          As

L'air devenu ſerein, il part tout morfondu,
Sèche du mieux qu'il peut ſon corps chargé de pluie.
Dans un champ à l'écart voit du bléd répandu,
Voit un Pigeon auprès, cela luî donné envie:
Il y vole, il eſt pris: ce bléd couvroit d'un las,
 Les menteurs & traîtres appâts.

    B 3   Le

As the threads were but rotten, he manag'd fo well,
    That he broke through tne murderous tackle,
As rejoic'd as a felon efcap'd from his cell,
    Though dragging his leg in a fhackle.

Again flapping his wings, and preparing for flight,
    Free from danger we cannot pronounce him :
Too foon was he feen by the quick-fighted kite,
    Who was inftantly ready to pounce him ,

But, in pity to Venus, benevolent Jove
    Difappointed the blood-thirfty finner,
Sent his eagle to refcue the favourite dove,
    Though he robb'd the poor kite of his dinner.

Our

Le las étoit ufé, fi bien que de fon aîle,
De fes piéds, de fon bec, l'oifeau le rompt enfin .
Quelque p¹u ne y périt; & le pis du deftin
Fut que un certain Vautour à la ferre cruelle,
Vit notre malheureux, qui traînant la ficelle,
Et les morceaux du las qui l'avoit attrappé,
    Sembloit un forçat échappé

Le

Our fugitive, after a very fhort flight,

 Next drops on the thatch of a cottage,

Expecting to reft, and recover his fright;

 But a boy, who was blowing his pottage,

Soon threw down his difh and his fpoon; for in truth,

 As misfortune and ill-luck would have it,

This pitilefs, cruel, but dexterous Youth,

 Was great grand-fon to little King David:

The Pigeon, more lucky, 'tis true, than Goliah,

 Receiv'd not its death from a fling,

But it certainly would, had the boy but been nigher,

 Who broke both a leg and a wing.

         Now

Le Vautour s'en alloit le lier, quand des nues

Fond à fon tour un Aigle aux aîles étendues.

Le Pigeon profita du conflit des voleurs,

S'envola, s'abattit auprès d'une mazure,

 Crut pour ce coup que fes malheurs

 Finnoient par cette aventure

Mais un fripon d'enfant, cet âge eft fans pitié,

Prit fa fronde, & d'un coup, tua plus d'amotié

 La volatille malheureufe,

   B 4   Qui

Now limping, alas ! with one leg in a ſtring,

    And lamenting and curſing his fate,

And trailing along with his poor broken wing,

    He return'd from his travels too. late.

He might have far'd worſe, 'midſt ſuch dangers beſet :

    With good nurſing he ſtill may recover,   -

Though wounded ſo much ; with what pleaſure they me

    No language of mine can diſcover.

Now let every ſenſible lover declare,

    If he wiſhes to wander or rove ;

Unleſs 'tis in ſearch of his favourite fair,

    Whom he'll meet in the neighbouring grove ;

                                And

Qui maudiſſant ſa curioſité,

    Trainant l'aîle, & tirant le pïéd,

    Demi morte, & demi boiteuſe,

    Droit au logis s'en retourna :

    Que bien que mal elle arriva,

    Sans autre aventure fâcheuſe.

Voilà, nos gens réjoints , & je laiſſe à juger

De combien de plaiſirs ils payerent leurs peins.

Amans, heureux amans, voulez vous voyager ?

    Que ce ſoit aux rives prochains.

                             Soyez

And with whom, fhould the delicate, dear blufhing maid
    Give confent, he'll triumphantly fpeed,
On galloping Hymen's poft-horfes convey'd,
    To *the pleafanter banks of the Tweed.*

In purfuit of fantaftical pleafure,
    After this, fhould they carelefsly roam,
They will forfeit an exquifite treafure,
    No where to be found but at home ;

A more precious and beautiful gem
    Than contentment, they ne'er can difcover ;
All the world will be nothing to them,
    If fincerely they love one another.

                        I formerly

Soyez-vous l'un à l'autre un monde toujours beau,
    Toujours divers, toujours nouveau :
Tenez-vous lieu de tout, comptez pour rien le refte.

                        J'ai

I formerly once was delighted,

   And liv'd amidft paftoral fcenes,

More happy than had I been knighted,

   In favour with Kings and their Queens.

Up the mountains, and over the plains,

   With dear liberty ftill did I rove;

Yet I boafted to wear her foft chains,

   As a flave to my *queen of the grove*,

The gay court, with its glittering treafure,

   And all the bright ftars in the fky,

Could afford me not half fo much pleafure,

   As a glance from *dear Phyllis's eye.*

                        Sh

J'ai quelquefois aimé   je n'aurois pas alors,

   Contre le Louvre & fes trélors,

Contre le Firmament & fa voûte célefte,

   Changé les bois, changé les lieus,

Honorés par les pas, éclairés par les yeux

   De l'aimable & jeune Bergère,

   Pour qui, fous le fils de Cythère,

Je fervis engagé par mes premiers fermens.

                        Hélas!

She was fairest where thousands are fair—

 But all thofe happy moments are fled ;

'Tis with exquifite grief I declare

 Difcontentednefs reigns in their ftead ;

For old father Time, with his forrowful face,

 Is telling Hymen his torch cannot burn ;

That the mind can paft moments of pleafure re-trace,

 But, alas ! they can never return.

THE

Hélas ! Quand reviendront de femblables momens ?
Faut-il que tant d'objets fi doux & fi chaimans,
Me laiflent vivre au gré de mon ame inquicte ?
Ah ! fi mon cœur ofoit encoi fe ienflammei !
Ne fentirai-je plus de charme qui m'arrête ?
  Ai-je pafſé le temps d'annei ?

Le

The CAT, the WEASEL, and the LITTLE RABBET.

EVER ready to feize all,
A witch of a Weafel,
With impudent fecrefy ftole,
One very fine morning,
Without giving warning,
Into poor little Bob Rabbet's hole:

Invit

Le Chat, la Belette, & le Petit Lapin.

DU palais d'un jeune Lapin
Dame Belette, un beau matin,
S'empara. c'eft une rufée.

Le

Invited by Flora,

As well as Aurora,

The dear little Buck had fat out,

From his happy domain,

Which he meant to regain,

After browfing and trotting about:

But when he got home,

Where he had but one room,

The fly flut whom I mention'd before,

With her nofe at the window,

Attempted to hinder

The Rabbet, who knock'd at the door:

Who,

Le Maître étant abfent, ce lui fut chofe aifée.

Elle porta chez lui fes Penates un jour

Qu'il étoit allé faire à l'Aurore fa cour,

Parmi le thim & la rofée.

Après qu'il eut brouté, trotté, fais tous fes tours,

Janot Lapin retourne aux foûterrains féjours.

La Belette avoit mis le nez à la fenêtre.

O dieux

Who the devil is here?

Says the young Pioneer.

Why, you vile little moufe-hunting ftrumpet!

So, Madam, you pleafe,

My caftle to feize,

Without formally founding the trumpet!

By my foul, fays the Rabbet,

I'll inftantly blab it;

I'll tell all the boys of your hole:

I'll point out the furrow

Which leads to the burrow,

Conducting myfelf the patrole.

Y

O Dieux hofpitaliers, que vois je ici paroître?

Dit l'animal chaffé du paternel logis:

Holà, Madame la Belette!

Que l'on déloge fans trompette,

Ou je vais avertir tous les Rats du pays.

You may do what you will,
I fhall here remain ftill;
And the door, Sir—I'll never unlock it—
No, Sir—you're miftaken—
You've your houfehold-gods taken—
'Tis a pity you had a fide-pocket.

And fhe turn'd up her nofe,
As you may fuppofe,
Declaring (as cuftom decrees it)
That the burrow was hers,
And this fhe avers,
As belonging to thofe who could feize it.

'Tis

La Dame au nez pointu répondit, que la terre
Etoit au premier occupant.

C'étoit

'Tis well worth a while

To talk in this ftyle,

And make a ridiculous pother,

'Bout a hole under ground,

Which was empty when found ;

You can eafily fcratch out another :

But, for argument's fake,

Will you juft undertake

To prove, Sir, who granted the leafe ?

Says the Rabbet, 'tis mine ;

For 'twas I paid the fine

Juft after my father's deceafe :

Yo

C'étoit un beau fujet de guerre,

Qu'un logis où lui-même il n'entroit qu'en rampant

Et quand ce feroit un Royaume

Je voudrois bien favoir, dit elle, qu'elle loi

En a pour toujours fait l'octroi

A Jean fils ou neveu de Pierre, ou de Guillaume,

Plûtôt qu'à Paul, plûtôt qu'à moi.

Jean Lapin allégua la coûtume & l'ufage.

Ce font, dit-il, leurs loix qui m'ont de ce logis

Rendu maître & Seigneur, & qui de pere en fils,

L'ori

You muſt alter your tone ;

This is certainly one

Of our family burrows—we've had 'em,

As hiſtory ſhews,

And all the world knows,

Since the time of our Grandfather Adam.

And to prove 'tis not thine,

But in equity mine,

That my title exhibits no flaw,

And with eaſe to ſubdue

Such vermin as you,

We'll appeal, if you pleaſe, to the law.

I'm

L'ont de Pierre à Simon, puis a moi Jean tranſmis,

Le premier occupant eſt-ce une loi plus ſage ?

Or bien ſans crier davantage,

C   Rapportons-

I'm by no means afraid

The complaint fhould be laid

Before my Lord Chancellor Scratch-all;

Now my Lord —— was a Cat,

Moft enormoufly fat,

Drefs'd up in a wig;——with a fatchel

He held in his claw,

Like a limb of the law:

But my Lord very feldom ftirr'd out,

Unlefs when a Moufe

Was approaching his houfe,

Where he liv'd like a hermit devout.

Togethe

Rapportons-nous, dit-elle, à Raminagrobis.

C'étoit un Chat vivant comme un dévot hermite;

Un Chat faifant la Chatemite,

Un faint homme de Chat, bien fourré, gros & gras,

Arbitre expert fur tous les cas.

Jean Lapin pour Juge l agrée.

Le

Together they trudge

To this excellent Judge:

Whilst his Reverence open'd the door,

(So loaded with fur

That he scarcely could stir)

Both his upright decision implore.

His whiskers stroaking first—he bow'd,

With reverential tread;

With dignity their suit approv'd,

And bow'd—but shook his head.

Approach, my children, said the sage,

With grave and solemn face;

Infirm, alas! and deaf with age,

I cannot hear the cafe.

They

Les voilà tous deux arrivées

Devant la Majesté fourré.

Grippeminaud leur dit : Mes enfans, approchez,

Approchez : je suis sourd, les ans en font la caufe.

L'un

They nearer came—and twice he hem'd,
    And thrice *he purr'd applaufe* ;
Whilft both were fecretly condemn'd
    To velvet-hidden claws ;

        With which they were feiz'd,
        And inhumanly fqueez'd—
    For the vile hypocritical finner
        His pleaders nonfuited,
        And ftomach recruited,
    By fnapping 'em up for his dinner.

THE

L'un & l'autre approcha, ne craignant nulle chofe.
Auffi-tôt qu'à portée il vit les conteftans,
        Grippeminaud, le bon apôtre,
Jettant des deux côtés la griffe en même temps,
Mit les Plaideurs d'accord en croquant l'un & l'autre.

THE RAT RETIRED FROM THE WORLD.

UPON the truth of all Legends we fhall not infift;
　　Though we cannot—no matter for that.
Mongft the lives of fome Saints, once crept into the lift
　　The Life of a Reverend Rat.

This world and its cares, all things under the moon,
　　He refign'd—whilft he liv'd at his eafe ,
And no wonder, indeed, for the Pious Poltroon
　　Was fhut up in a fine Chefhire cheefe.

　　　　　　　　　　　　　　　Thus

Le Rat qui s'eft retiré du Monde.

LES Lévantines, en leur Légende,
　　Difent qu'un certain Rat, las des foins d'ici-bas,
Dans un fromage de Hollande
Se retira loin du tracas.

　　　　　　　　　　La

Thus did Monks who were cloifter'd in lazinefs lurk,
  Till an Emperor's recent command,
Decreed, that thofe fubjects who never would work,
  Should not live on the fat of the land :

All the year if fad mortals in cloifters delight,
  Nor enjoy the fweet change of the feafons,
They like darknefs, undoubtedly, better than light;
  But not without infamous reafons :

For in houfes religious, we readily own,
  Are finners fometimes to be found .
Like cheefes, they're rotten within, 'tis well known,
  Though their roofs and their fides remain found.

I thought

La folitude étoit profonde,
S'entendant par tout à la ronde.
Notre Hermite nouveau fubfiftoit là-dedans.

I thought we with safety might make a digression,
    And return to the Rat—he's at home:
Who could think of relinquishing such a possession,
    Any longer intending to roam?

Contented we left him, contented we find him,
    In his Hermitage happily quiet;
For, enlarging his cell both before and behind him,
    He wanted nor lodging nor diet:

His Reverence never neglecting his meat,
    And in safety forgetting the Cat,
Without exercise living within his retreat,
    Soon became most enormously fat.

After

Il fit tant des piéds & des dents,
Qu'en peu de jours il eût au fond de l'hermitage
Le vivre & le couvert. Que faut-il davantage?
Il devint gros & gras: Dieu prodigue ses biens
A ceux qui font vœu d'être siens.

C 4

Un

After dinner one day was he taking his nap,
 As was always his cuftom to do ;
When fome ftrange running-footmen began with a rap,
 And then rattled——a-rat-a-tat-too.

His Grace almoft afleep—juft beginning to fnore,
 Started up at the people's approach ;
When a foreign Ambaffador drove to the door,
 And politely ftept out of his coach ;—

Ratopolis, Sir, is attack'd—from the Rats
 I'm deputed to tell you, my Liege,
That the *Duke de Grimalkin*, with ten thoufand Cats,
 On his march, will foon open the fiege.

'Mongft

Un jour au dévot perfonage,
Des députés du peuple Rat
S'en vinrent demander quelque aumône légère .
Ils alloient en terre étrangère,
Chercher quelque fecours cortre le peuple Chat :
Ratopolis étoit bloquée ;

10

 On

'Mongft his troops are few kittens, except fome French-
    frifkers,
  With diamond buttons and loops in their hats;
The reft are all grenadiers, with long terrible whifkers,
    Well-difciplin'd—veteran Cats.

To be brief—the ftate begs that, without any quibble,
    Your Holinefs inftantly fend her
Some ftores, without which, having nothing to nibble,
    The garrifon foon muft furrender:

Hanoverian fuccours of every kind
    Are expected—as yet we've not got 'em;
In every fhip, befides cafh, we fhall find
    A Battalion of Rats in its bottom:

                      But

On les avoit contraints de partir fans argent,
    Attendu l'état indigent
    De la République attaquée.

But at prefent, I fay, without better finances,
    Expences cannot be defray'd ;
And a loan which your Reverend Worfhip advances,
    Shall with intereft foon be repaid.

My dear friends, reply'd the religious Reclufe,
    Tell the ftate (yet it grieves me to tell 'em)
From the world I retir'd can prove of no ufe,
    Though forry for what has befel 'em,

That long fince have I fworn not to leave my retreat :
    That an indigent Hermit declares,
Though nought he can give, for the good of the ftate,
    Yet he'll ardently pour forth his prayers.

'Twas

Ils demandoient fort peu, certains que le fecours
    Seroit prêt dans quatre ou cinque jours,
    Mes amis, dit le Solitaire,
Les chofes d'ici-bas ne me regardent plus :
    En quoi peut un pauvre Reclus
    Vous affifter ? Que peut-il faire,
Que de prier le Ciel qu'il vous aide en ceci ?

J'efpère

'Twas all th' Ambaſſador got, with his humble retinue,
    Their ſinking Republic to prop;
For, determin'd their talk ſhould no longer continue,
    The Cheeſemonger ſhut up his ſhop.

                      T H E

J eſpère qu'il aura de vous quelque ſouci.
    Ayant parlé de cette ſorte,
    Le nouveau Saint ferma ſa porte.

                      La

The PIGEON and the ANT.

A PIGEON obferv'd, as fhe ftoop'd at the brink,
    A poor Ant overwhelm'd in the ftream ;
Tho' thirfty, yet never a drop would fhe drink
    Till fhe'd plann'd her benevolent fcheme :

Indulging her thirft—fhe'd have been but too late,
    So long had fhe ftruggled in vain,
That it ne'er could have been the poor Labourer's fate,
    The rivulet's edge to regain.

Away

La Colombe & la Fourmi.

L E long d'un clau ruiffeau bûvoit une Colombe ·
    Quand fur l'eau fe penchant une Fourmis y tombe,
Et dans cet Océan l'on eût vû la Fourmis
S efforcer, mais en vain, de regagner la rive.

La

Away fhe flew—but return'd with a branch in her bill

   (Again an emblem of life's reftauration)

Which was inftantly plac'd with fuch exquifite fkill,

   That it ferv'd as a bridge of falvation ;

Whilft heaven-born *Pity* ftood near as a guide,

   (If loft left the ftate fhould bewail her)

'Twas a *Cape of Good Hope*, which with joy fhe defcry'd,

   Like * Inglefield's extatic failor.

She with eagernefs try'd, the firft moment fhe landed,

   To reach the republican neft ;

But *Pity's Sifter* ftood one of the group, and demanded,

   In *Gratitude*'s name, an arreft ;

Pointing

* See Inglefield's Narrative.

La Colombe, auffi-tôt ufé de charité,
Un brin de herbe dans l'eau par elle étant jetté,
Ce fut un Promontoire où la Fourmis arrive.
    Elle fe fauve ; & là-deffus
Paffe un certain Croquant, qui marchoit les piéds nuds :

Cc

Pointing out to the reptile the Game-keeper's gun,
 Which he'd level'd, unerringly fkill'd ,
In a moment the murderous deed had been done,
 And Venus's favourite kill'd :

For already the Villain (fuppofing he'd got her)
 Within himfelf fecretly boafted
(Whilft licking his lips) that fhe fhou'd, when he'd fhot her,
 Soon be moft delicioufly roafted ;

And he tickled the trigger—yet willing to fteal,
 If poffible, nearer—the Sinner
Started up—for the reptile was biting his heel—
 When away flew the Dove, and his dinner.

T H I

Ce Croquant par hazard avoit un arbalête.
 Dès qu'il voit l'Oifeau de Venus,
Il le croit en fon pot, & déjà lui fait fête.
Tandis qu'à le tuer mon Villageois s'apprête,
 La Fourmi le pique au talon.
 Le Vilain retourne la tête,
La Colombe l'entend, part, & tire de la long.
 Le foupé du Croquant avec elle s'envole :
 Point de Pigeon pour une obole.

Le

The ANIMALS SICK OF THE PLAGUE.

TO punish every quadruped,
    And favourite mortals spare,
Once Jupiter let loose ('tis said)
    His angry dogs of war.

Fierce Sirius beam'd with violence,
    His fiery rage increas'd,
And pestilential influence
    Infected every beast;

Of

Les Animaux malades de la Peste.

UN mal qui répand la terreur
    Mal que le Ciel, en sa fureur,
Inventa pour punir les crimes de la terre,
La Peste (puisqu'il faut l'appeller par son nom)

Capable

Of this the Dog below appriz'd,

His three mouths open'd wide;

But Cerberus was tantaliz'd,

For few there were that died:

Death not his darts—but threat'nings dealt;

To ftrike he ftill refrains;

Whilft every languid creature felt

The poifon in his veins:

Their lives no longer to fuftain

Were various fchemes concerted,

Defpairing they forfook the plains,

And defarts were deferted:

Poor

Capable d'enrichir en un jour l'Acheron,

Faifoit aux Animaux la guerre.

Ils ne mouroient pas tous, mais tous étoit frappés.

On n'en voyoit point d'occupés

A chercher le foutien d'une mourante vie:

Nul mets n'excitoit leur envie.

M

Poor Pufs (fcarce wifhing it) efcapes
 Diftemper'd Dogs let loofe ;
The feverifh Fox ftill longs for grapes,
 But loaths the lingering Goofe :

Each other to relinquifh forc'd,
 In melancholy tone,
Poor amorous Turtles, felf-divorc'd,
 Reciprocally mourn.

A council now the Lion calls :
 Weak limbs but ill fupport
Each Senator, who feebly crawls,
 Though fcarce alive, to court.

To

Ni Loups, ni Renards, n'épioient
La douce & l'innocente proie.
Les Tourterelles fe fuyoient :
Plus d'amour, paitant plus de joie.

To whom, when met, the Royal Sage—
    We murderers here on earth
Our angry Gods muſt try t'aſſuage,
    And deprecate their wrath:

All Heaven a willing ear may lend,
    (Our prayer if Pity ſings)
" Some reconciling Saint to ſend,
    " With healing in his wings."

With truth th' hiſtoric page is fraught:
    From thence, by virtuous Fate,
Of ſelf-devoted victims taught,
    We'll ſave the ſinking ſtate.

Though

Le Lion tint conſeil, & dit=Mes chers amis,
    Je croi que le Ciel a permis
    Pour nos péchés cette infortune:
    Que le plus coupable de nous
Se ſacrifie aux traits du céleſte courroux.
Peut-être il obtiendra la guériſon commune.
L'hiſtoire nous apprend qu'en de tels accidens
    On fait de pareils dévoûmens.

Though frequently, to hide our faults,
　　Self-flattery draws the veil ;
If confciences at crimes revolt,
　　Confeffions muft prevail.

In what have Sheep offended ?
　　Yet I, voracious glutton !
My greedy guts diftended,
　　When I could dine on mutton

But yet, what's worfe to tell, at laft,
　　By appetite untoward
Induc'd to vary the repaft,
　　The Shepherd I've devour'd :

If

Ne nous flattons donc point, voyons fans indulgence
　　L'état de notre confcience.
Pour moi, fatisfaifant mes appétits gloutons,
　　J'ai dévoré force Moutons
　　Que m'avoient-ils fait ?　Nulle offenfe :
Même il m'eft arrivé quelquefois de manger le Berger.

If guilty moſt, I'll not refuſe
    Moſt willingly to die ;
But firſt, let every one accuſe
    Himſelf, as well as I.

The Fox, though dying, ſtill a Knave,
    Says—What a happy thing
It is, when loyal ſubjeċts have
    An equitable King !

Though now and then you've kill'd a Sheep,
    And then have din'd upon her;
Poor ſimpletons ! no longer weep,
    You did 'em too much honour:

Fo

Je me dévoûrai donc, s'il le faut   mais je penſe
Qu'il eſt bon que chacun s'accuſe ainſi que moi,
Car ont doit ſouhaiter, ſelon tout juſtice,
    Que le plus coupable périſſe.
Sire, dit le Renard, vous étes trop bon Roi ;
Vos ſcrupules font voir trop de délicateſſe ;
Et bien, manger moutons, canaille, ſotte eſpece !
Eſt-ce un pêché ? Non, non ; vous leur fîtes, Seigneur,
    En les croquant beaucoup d'honneur.

For trifling crimes no King atones ;

  The Sheep fhould be forgotten,

They poffibly were Aged Crones,

  And probably were rotten.

'Twas right to take the Shepherd's life,

  More cruel than his Dog ;

For every month the Monfter's knife

  Cuts up the Bacon Hog.

To pleafe the Monarch every word

  And fyllable confpir'd ,

The Flatterer's fpeech the wicked herd

  Of murderers admir'd.

         Each

Et quant au Berger, l'on peut dire

  Qu'il étoit digne de tous maux ,

Etant de ces gens-là qui, fur les Animaux,

  Se font un chimérique empire.

Ainfi, dit le Renard, & flatteurs d'applaudir .

  On n'ofa trop approfondir

Du Tigre, ni de l'Ours, ni des autres Puiffances

  Les moins pardonnables offenfes.

Each t'other to confeffion mov'd,

    Great crimes were fmall complaints;

Self-advocates, themfelves they prov'd

    A *calendar of Saints.*

When all the vile carnivorous clan,

    Bears, Wolves, and Dogs, had done;

The long-ear'd Animal began,

    And thus addrefs'd the throne:

Since other beafts do theirs confefs,

    My crimes I cannot hide;

But if they greater are, or lefs,

    Let Equity decide.

                          Once,

Tous les gens querelleurs, jufqu'aux fimples Mâtins,
Au dire de chacun, étoient de petits Saints.
L'Ane vint à fon tour, & dit: J ai fouvenance
    Qu'en un pré de Moines paffant,

Once, almoſt fainting with a load
    I'd carried many a mile,
Me, meeting in the duſty road,
    Some Devil did beguile :

The green-rob'd meadow's waving pride
    The pamper'd Horſe may paſs ;
But, hungry Wretch ! I ſtep'd aſide,
    And ſtole a little graſs ;

I'd ſcarcely got a mouthful, when
    The Gardener's Boy, my Maſter,
Soon turn'd me tow'rds the road again,
    And made me travel faſter .

                      At

La faim, l'occaſion, l'herbe tendre, & je penſe,
    Quelque Diable auſſi me pouſſant,
Je tondis de ce pré la largeur de ma langue.

At market he was meafuring out
On one fide peafe and beans;
On t'other fide I turn'd my fnout,
And ftole a bunch of greens.

A right to fteal I'll not difpute,
An apple yet I've ftole;
At other times not fond of fruit,
'Twas when I've been with foal.

Poor honeft Dapple! when fhe'd made
This innocent confeffion;
The wicked Wolf began t' upbraid
The triplicate tranfgreffion.

Attorney

Je n'en avois nul droit, puifqu'il faut parler net,
A ces mots on cria haro fur le Baudet.

Uı

Attorney-general to the Gang,

   He partially declaims ;

And with an infamous harangue,

   The multitude inflames :

Examples, e'en celeftial, prove

   Our bloody deeds are right ;

The fanguinary Gods above

   In facrifice delight :

But hateful to the Deities

   Are daily crimes like thefe ;

For, though not great enormities,

   Continually they difpleafe.

                       The

Un Loup, quelque peu Clerc, prouva par fa harangue,

Qu'il falloit devouer ce maudit animal,

Ce pelé, ce galeux, d'où venoit tout le mal.

The nature of the Culprit's crime
　　Judiciously survey;
Of grafs one mouthful makes, in time,
　　At leaft a trufs of hay:

This Afs devour'd, perhaps, a load,
　　Deftroy'd it in the bud;
But if the thief had kept the road,
　　The Farmer's grafs had ftood:

His hopes of harveft to deftroy
　　'Twas wicked and unjuft;
But, when fhe robb'd the Gard'ner's Boy,
　　'Twas then a breach of truft.

The

The Gard'ner's clamorous Wife, no doubt,
    The carelefs Boy would thrafh,
When, fniveling, he return'd without
    His complement of cafh:

What's worfe — whilft various thefts pervert
    Her appetite, the Brute,
As if afham'd of a defert,
    Pretends to long for fruit.

I wonder that the fnout dar'd tell,
    With neatnefs it could whip in,
Perhaps the noble Nompareil,
    Perhaps the Golden Pippin.

Succefsfully

Succefsfully the Wolf harangu'd :

  Poor felf-indiＣted Dapple

Was try'd—condemn'd at laſt—and hang'd,

  Becauſe ſhe ſtole an apple.

Tᴴᴱ

Sa peccadille fut jugée un cas pendable.

Manger l'herbe d'autrui !　Quel crime abominable !

  Rien que la mort n'étoit capable

D'expier fon forfait . on le lui fit bien voir.

L

The YOUNG WIDOW.

THOUGH lamented the marry'd man dies,
    Whilst to grieve the poor Wife perseveres;
On the wings of old Time Sorrow flies,
    And his course turns the tide of her tears:

The Wife who's been widow'd a day,
    Has already shed many a tear:
Of her sorrows but what shall we say,
    Whose Husband departed last year?

                            With

La Jeune Veuve.

LA perte d'un Epoux ne va point sans soupirs.
    On fait beaucoup de bruit, & puis on se console.
Sur les aîles du Temps la Tristesse s'envole,
      Le Temps ramène les plaisirs.
      Entre la Veuve d'une année,
      Et la Veuve d'une journée,

                            La

With the fits of the firſt are tormented

 Thoſe friends who dare viſit poor Madam;

Of which t'other long ſince has repented,

 And indeed is aſtoniſh'd ſhe had 'em.

Try not with the firſt to prevail;

 But let her alone—'tis as well

To diſcredit her ſorrowful tale,

 And attend to the ſtory I'll tell.—

A Huſband who once had a beautiful Wife

Was, to ſee t'other world, ſetting out;

But as 'twas on a ſudden he quitted this life,

He ſent home for his wife——from a Route;

         Who,

La différence eſt grande. On ne croiroit jamais

 Que ce fût la même perſonne.

· L un fait fuir les gens, & l'autre à mille attraits:

Aux ſoupirs vrais ou faux celle-là s'abandonne:

C eſt toujours même note, & pareil entretien:

  On dit, qu'on eſt inconſolable:

  On le dit, mais il n'en eſt rien,

  Comme on verra par cette Fable,

  Ou plutôt par la vérité.

  L'Epoux d'un jeune Beauté

Partoit pour l'autre monde. A ſes côtés ſa Femme

    3   Lui

Who, though she was winning a *Sans-prendre Vole*,
   The *Miraculous Draught* difregards ;
The poor forrowful creature no gains could confole,
   She diftractedly threw down the cards :

At home, in a moment, she flew to the bed,
   Nor regarded her friends who ftood by;
After wringing her hands, she got hold of his head,
   Declaring——You never shall die ;

If you do, I shall follow th' example of thofe
   Who feldom their Hufbands furvive ;
But, as foon as he's dead, will let none interpofe,
   If they choofe to be roafted alive.

                              She

Lui croit : Attens-moi, je te fuis, & mon ame,

                                  Auffi-bien

She fear'd not (she protested) Death's terrible dart,

    When——the good man went off in a groan ;

And though quite ready, the moment before, to depart,

    She thought he might as well travel alone.

Her father prudently meant not at first to reproach her,

    Discommending immoderate grief ;

Yet, cautiously kind, when the storm was blown over,

    Prescrib'd consolation's relief.

'Tis too much, said the tender Old Man, my Dear Daughter,

    The Dead Man can no benefit reap,

Though, lamenting him still, you shed rivers of water

    From those eyes which incessantly weep :

                  You're

Aussi-bien que la tienne, est prête à s'envoler,

    Le Mari fait seul le voyage.

La Belle avoit un père, homme prudent & sage :

    Il laissa le torrent couler.

    A la fin, pour la consoler,

Ma fille, lui dit il, c'est trop verser de larmes :

Qu'à besoin le défunt que vous noyiez vos charmes ?

                  Puisqu'i

You're a victim devoted, whom Envy beguiles,
    Left your brightnefs once more fhould appear;
To prevent it you've cruelly delug'd your fmiles,
    And ev'ry dimple fill'd up with a tear:

Too foon that fome Widows, I cannot but own,
    Their tears moft indecently fmother;
And in hafte, having bury'd one Hufband to-day,
    To-morrow run after another:

Yet in time, if I fhould, my dear Daughter, propofe—
    He was gently proceeding to tell her
That the Youth whom he'd anxioufly thought of, and chofe,
    Was an elegant handfome young fellow;

                       But

Puifqu'il eft des vivans, ne fongez plus aux morts.
    Je ne dis pas que tout à-l'heure
    Une condition meilleure,
    Change en des nôces ces tranfports.
Mais après certain temps, fouffrez qu'on vous propofe
Un Epoux beau, bien fait, jeune, & tout autre chofe

            E   Que

But a greater ftorm the poor Father could not have prefag'd
 Had he tender'd an old barrel'd oyfter :
With indignation fhe turn'd up her nofe, and enrag'd,
 Swore fhe'd finifh her days in a cloifter.

The Father, made cautious, defifted a while,
 Having fuffer'd a month to elapfe;
When Madam, thinking to drefs in a different ftyle,
 Now began to look over her caps :

Ev'ry day produc'd fome alteration in drefs,
 Which at prefent the Dame could adorn :
Yet, as decency's rules fhe difdain'd to tranfgrefs,
 Only black-and-white flounces were worn.

A,

Que le défunt. Ah! dit-elle auffi-tôt,
 Un Cloître eft l'Epoux qu'il me faut.
Le Pere lui laiffa digérer fa difgrace.
 Un mois de la foite fe paffe.
L'autre mois, on l'emploie à changer tous les jours
Quelque chofe à l'habit, au linge, à la coeffure.

Le

As engravings, depriv'd of th' original's tint,
   Are often approv'd of as fuch;
So fhe was efteem'd like an excellent print,
   And by judges admir'd as much :

But at laft, when full blown, in her colours appear'd
   The bright morning-ftar of Dame Nature,
All judges, without hefitation, averr'd
   Titian drefs'd out the beautiful creature.

That her conquefts again fhould extend far and wide,
   She was always in battle array,
And look'd (all her forrowful weeds laid afide)
   Like a Butterfly born on May-day.

                                    In

Le deuil enfin fert de parure,
En attendant d'autres atouis,

In abundance new Lovers fubmitted to fate,
 Befides old ones, and five or fix Coufins;
With fifty tongues I their numbers could never relate,
 For the poor fouls died by dozens and dozens.

Her houfe with fad victims was conftantly fill'd,
 Who certain deftruction were wooing
So fometimes in a dove-houfe are poor Pigeons kill'd,
 Where a Cat puts an end to their cooing.

Poor creatures! and can we their conduct upbraid,
 Who died, 'caufe they thought there was wit in
Their Cat, which refembled a Venus, and play'd
 Foolifh tricks, like a frolickfome kitten?

But

Toute la bande des Amours
Revient au Colombier. les jeux, les ris, la danfe,
Ont auffi leur tour à la fin.

On

But to finifh my fable—From morning till night
   Dear pleafure bewitches her throng :
When numbers have led down the dance with delight,
   Simple melody warbles her fong ;

Then long-winded Fifcher withholds the foft note,
   Which dies away—then returns like a breeze ;
And, as foon as he's done, all the company vote
   To finifh with catches and glees.

That the Hufband fhe formerly had was forgot,
   Now the Father was fecretly certain ;
And though the marriage-bed was moft undoubtedly not—
   He would not mention fo much as its curtain ,

                                           But

     On fe plonge, fou & matin,
       Dans la fontaine de Jouvence.
   Le Pere ne craint plus ce défunt tant chéri :
   Mais comme il ne parloit de rien à notre Belle ;

But was dumb for a month—till his dear Daughter Anne,

    Not wishing much longer to tarry,

Said—Which, Sir, of my Beaux is the beautiful Man;

    The Man whom you'd wish me to marry ?

T H E

Où donc est le jeune Mari

Que vous m'avez promis ? dit-elle,

The YOUNG COCK, the CAT, and the LITTLE MOUSE.

A POOR little Moufe,
    Which was bred in the houfe,
Stole abroad, and fet off on his travels;
    Without prudence or thought,
    But was near being caught,
As the tale he related unravels:

Trotting

***

Le Cochet, le Chat, & le Souriceau.

UN Souriceau tout jeune, & qui n'avoit rien vû,
    Fut prefque pris au dépourvû.
Voici comme il conta l'aventure à fa Mère.

E 4

J'avois

Trotting on, fays the Brat,

As bold as a Rat,

Who rambles abroad at his pleafure,

I met with two Creatures,

Whofe different features

Surpriz'd me, Mama, beyond meafure :

To be cringingly kind

The one was inclin'd,

With a countenance mild and demure ;

But fo turbulent, Mother,

And noify was t'other,

His behaviour I could not endure :

If

J'avois franchi les Monts qui bornent cet Etat ;

Et trottois, comme un jeune Rat

Qui cherche à fe donner carrière,

Lorfque deux Animaux m'ont arrêté les yeux :

L'un doux, benin, & gracieux,

Et l'autre turbulent, & plein d'inquiétude.

Il

If I do not miftake,

A bit of beef-fteak

Mr. Impudence had on his head,

As if intended for fale

And, hung out at his tail

A bunch of fine feathers were fpread.

But how did I ftare,

When with arms in the air,

He lifted himfelf from the ground;

Setting up fuch a roar,

As I think heretofore

Never made frighten'd Echo refound !

Then

Il a la voix perçante & rude :

Sur la tête un morceau de chair,

Une forte de bras dont il s'éleve en l'air,

Comme pour prendre fa volée,

La queue en panache étalée.

Or c'étoit un Cochet dont notre Souriceau

Fit à fa Mère le tableau,

Comme d un Animal venu de l'Amérique.

Il fe battoit, dit-il, les flancs avec fes bras,

Faifant tel bruit, & tel fracas.

Que

Then beating his fides,

And advancing—he ftrides,

With intention, no doubt, to affail;

But I fcamper'd away,

And avoided the fray,

Very prudently turning my tail ·

Without a retreat,

But a mouthful of meat

The magnanimous Monfter had gain'd;

You'd have certainly got

Dame Niobe's lot,

Nor my terrible lofs have fuftain'd.

W

Que moi, qui grace aux Dieux, de courage me pique,

En ai pris le fuite de peur,

Le maudiffant de très-bon cœur

With regret I declare,
If there had not been there
This impertinent, riotous Devil,
An acquaintance I'd made
With t'other beautiful jade,
So apparently modeſt and civil ;

Whoſe glittering eyes
And playful tail would ſurpriſe
Thoſe who know not the velveted creature ;
With what pleaſure they'd doat
On her tortoiſe-ſhell coat,
Moſt enchantingly ſpotted by Nature !

Though

Sans lui j'aurois fait connoiſſance
Avec cet animal qui m'a ſemble ſi doux.
Il eſt velouté comme nous,
Marqueté, longue queue, un humble contenance,
Un modeſte regard, & pourtant l'œil luiſant.

Je

Though bigger by far

Than my Great-grand-mama,

Yet 'tis eafily feen by her ears

That this delicate Venus

Refembles our genus,

By their parallel fhape it appears.

Though ev'ry Moufe knows

The Cock's voice when he crows,

'Tis a meafure I'd always advife,

Says the Mother, to run;

And 'twas very well done,

You was ftill, Sir, more lucky than wife.

T'other

Je le crois fort fympatifant

Avec Meffieurs les Rats : car il a des oreilles

En figure aux notres pareilles.

J'allois aborder, quand, d'un fon plein d'éclat,

L'autre m'a fait prendre la fuite.

T'other creature fo fat

Was no lefs than the Cat;

Who, inftead of beef, mutton, and veal,

Is fo cruelly nice,

That fhe lives upon Mice,

Snapping up five or fix at a meal:

But foon the poor Cock

Will be brought to the block,

Where his innocent blood will be fhed;

Whilft in vain he'll upbraid

The bold hard-hearted Maid,

Whofe dexterity chops off his head:

Then

Mon Fils, dit la Souris, ce doucet eft un Chat,

Qui, fous fon minois hypocrite,

Contre toute ta parenté

D'un malin vouloir eft porté.

L'autre

Then with bacon and greens

He'll be boil'd, or French beans;

And what's nearer the bone will be left,

As a sweeter repast

For my Children at last,

Who'll deliciously sup on the theft.

From the countenance judge not;

Near hypocrites trudge not;

They're all smooth-fac'd, sly, simpering sinners,

Hadn't you better be picking

The bones of a Chicken,

Than snapp'd up by the Cat—for her dinner?

THE

L'autre Animal, tout au contraire,

Bien éloigné de nous mal faire,

Servira quelque jour peut-être à nos repas.

Quant au Cnat, c'est sur nous qu'il fonde sa cuisine.

Garde-toi, tant que tu vivras,

De juger les gens sur la mine.

4

The HERN.

A Long-legged Hern, in a bright summer's day,
　When the stream was enchantingly clear,
Stalk'd along, 's if intending the banks to survey,
　Like a Bridgewater's chief Engineer.

With deliberate step, and a quick-sighted eye,
　She could easily number the Fish;
And (one after another the tribes passing by)
　Might have pick'd out an excellent dish.

For

Le Héron.

UN jour, sur ses longs piéds alloit je ne sçais où,
　Le Héron au long bec emmanché d'un long cou.
　　Il côtoyoit une rivière.
L onde étant transparente, ainsi qu'aux plus beaux jours:

Ma

For whilft fly-catching Trouts the fmooth furface approac

    No longer conceal'd in the deep,

The Carp, with carelefs fecurity, follows the Roach,

    Not regarding the Pike faft afleep.

Th' hypocritical Lady pretended to faft,

    Her appetite firft was fo quiet;

And, notwithftanding fhe came to her ftomach at laft,

    Dainty Madam found fault with the diet;

Like Horace's whimfical Rat — who, forfooth,

    Could not fup on a piece of cold mutton,

With varieties cloy'd; whilft his dainty proud tooth

    Would fcarcely nibble a gingerbread button.

I came

Ma commère la Carpe y faifoit-mille tours

    Avec le Brochet fon compère.

L'Héron en eût fait aifément fon profit :

Tous approchoient du bord, l'Oifeau n'avoit qu'à prendre

    Mais il crut mieux faire d'attendre

    Qu'il eût un peu plus d'appétit.

Il vivoit de régîme; & mangeoit à fes heures.

Après quelques momens l'appétit vint : l'Oifeau

    S'approchant du bord, vit fur l'eau

Des Tanches qui fortoient du fond de ces demeures.

Le mets ne lui plut pas, il s'attendoit à mieux,

    Et montroit un goût dédaigneux,

    Comme le Rat du bon Horace.

Mo

I came not such paltry provisions to seek;

    Carp and Tench were not made for my gullet:

I'm determin'd I never will open my beak,

    For any thing less than a Mullet.

But no delicate Mullet, alas ! gliding by,

    (Since at last was her appetite sharp)

Refusing Gudgeons, and other diminutive fry,

    She condescended to long for a Carp :

'Twas too late in the day.   Not a fish could she see,

    For the stars were beginning to twinkle ;

And, lest she should go to bed supperless, she

    Gladly gulp'd down a poor Periwinkle.

                        From

Moi des Tanches ! dit-il, moi Heron que je fasse
Un si pauvre chére ? et pour qui me prend-on ?
La Tanche, rebutée, il trouva du Goujon
Du Goujon ! c'est bien là le dîner d'un Heron !
J'ouvrirois pour si peu le bec ! Aux Dieux ne plaise.
Il l'ouvrit pour bien moins: tout alla de façon
    Qu'il ne vit plus aucun poisson.
La faim le prit : il fut tout heureux, et tout aise
    De rencontrer un Limaçon.

From hence let Prudes a leſſon learn,
  Nor take th' advice in dudgeon,
Leſt, like the diſappointed Hern,
  They cannot get a Gudgeon.

* *In men's affairs there is a tide,*
  Which, taken at the flood,
Acts like a kind conducting guide,
  To lead them on to good:

But, if omitted once, 'tis found,
  The voyage of their life
Thenceforward is in ſhallows bound,
  And miſeries and ſtrife.

The

---

* Shakeſpear's Julius Cæſar

Ne ſoyons pas ſi difficiles ·
Les plus accommodans, ce ſont les plus habiles,
On hazard de perdre en voulant trop gagner.
  Gardez-vous de rien dédaigner,
Sur tout, quand vous avez à peu près votre compte.

Ben

The Damſel who long time delays
  Her choice, will be miſtaken ;
Too difficult, at laſt ſhe ſtays,
  To loſe the flitch of bacon.

THE

Bien des gens y ſont pris : ce n'eſt pas aux Herons
Que je parle : écoutez, Humains, un autre conte.
Vous verrez que chez vous j'ai puiſſé ces leçons.

F 2   La

The CAPRICIOUS LADY.

QUITE certain formerly, forfooth,
    The proud capricious Kitty
Pretended fhe could gain a Youth,
    Young, beautiful, and witty:

Agreeable, not frivolous,
    Like fome fantaftic fellows;
But all alive and amorous,
    And yet by no means jealous.

A

La Fille.

CERTAINE Fille, un peu trop fiére,
    Prétendoit trouver un Mari
Jeune, bien fait, et beau, d'agréable manière,
Point froid, et point jaloux : notez ces deux points ci.

Cett'

At firſt, attentive to the Maid,
    Dame Deſtiny was kind ;
And numbers ſent, in whom, 'twas ſaid,
    All virtues were combin'd.

Though Fortune did ſuch bleſſings bring,
    She made the Men retreat ;
With folly not confidering
    Mind, body, nor eſtate.

Firſt came ſome gilded Noblemen
    She ſoon made them retire ;
And then the golden Citizen,
    And then the Country 'Squire ,

                    The

Cette Fille vouloit auſſi
   Qu'il eût du bien, de la naiſſance,
De l'eſprit, enfin tout : mais qui peut tout avoir ʼ
Le Deſtin ſe montra ſoigneux de la pouvoir :
   Il vint des partis d'importance.
La Belle les trouva trop chétifs de moitié.

             Quoi

The Noble Puppies had no purfe;

  Cits had indeed refources,

But nothing elfe; whilft Hunters curfe,

  And talk of dogs and horfes.

Befides, if you'll obferve their looks,

  You'll *plainly* fee, the Graces,

Dame Nature's maids and paftry-cooks,

  Forgot to form their faces:

Undoubtedly my friends are mad,

  Such monfters to propofe;

One fquints, one grins, and one, egad!

  Has got but half a nofe;

           For,

Quoi moi? Quoi ces gens-là? L'on radote, je penfe,
A moi les propofer? Hélas! ils font pitié.
  Voyez un peu la belle efpéce!
L'un n'avoit en l'efprit nulle délicateffe,
L'autre avoit le nez fait de cette façon-là:

         C'étoit

For, wantonly to fhew their fkill,
  The giggling Girls had put on,
For one man's chin—a woodcock's bill,
  And for his nofe—a button.

Thefe, by the Damfel once difmifs'd,
  Returning not again;
She found but in her fecond lift,
  A moderate fet of men :

And, mad with difappointment, fwore
  Such folks fhould ne'er gain entry,
For ever fhe would fhut the door
  'Gainft fuch indifferent gentry.

With

C'étoit ceci, c'étoit cela,
  C'étoit tout, car les précieufes
  Font deffu tout les dédaigneufes,
Après les bons partis, les médiocres gens
  Vinrent fe mettre fur les rangs.
Elle de fe moquer, Ah, vraiment, je fuis bonne
De leur ouvrir la porte : ils penfent que je fuis

Fort

With impudence themfelves t'obtrude,
 What can fuch wretches mean?
My nights, though fpent in folitude,
 Are fpent without chagrin.

Difdainfully Coquettes proceed,
 Pretending they're content;
By Deftiny 'tis ftill decreed,
 In time they fhall repent.

Difquieted at laft, too late,
 Whilft years fucceed each other;
Alas ! poor difcontented Kate
 In time loft every Lover.

And

Fort en peine de ma perfonne.
Grace à Dieu, je paffe les nuits
Sans chagrin, quoiqu'en folitude.
La Belle fe fut gré de tous ces fentimens.
L'âge la ft déchoii   adieu tous les Amans.

Un

And whilft her favourite locks grew grey,
    And nofe put forth the pimple,
She found that every New-year's day
    Depriv'd her of a dimple.

Each feature chang'd the Nymph alarms,
    She tries to re-inftate 'em ;
Procuring, to repair her charms,
    Paint, powder, and pomatum :

And more fubftantial things fhe tries,
    Plump-cufhions and cork-rumps ;
Whilft with dexterity fhe ties
    New teeth to rotten ftumps.

                  A ruin'd

Un an fe paffe, & deux, avec inquiétude.
Le chagrin vient enfuivre . elle fent chaque jour
Déloger quelques Ris, quelques Jeux, puis l'Amour ;
    Puis fes traits choquer & déplaire :
Puis cents fortes de fards. Ses foins ne purent faire
Qu'elle échappât au Temps, cet infigne larron.

                  Les

A ruin'd houfe we foon repair

 By fending for a Mafon;

But to the face, which once was fair,

 When Kitty puts a cafe on,

Old father Time abhors the trade;

 Her pains fhe might have fpar'd:

What was created was not made,

 And cannot be repair'd:

A *moral truth* — which to pronounce,

 And kindly recommend,

The Mirror trys — her favourite once,

 And ftill her faithful friend.

DIALOGUE.

Les ruines d'une maifon

Se peuvent réparer: que n'eft cet avantage

 Pour les ruines du vifage!

Sa préciofité changea lors de langage.

Son Miroir lui difoit: Prenez vîte un Mari;

Je

DIALOGUE.

Looking-Glass. You once knew many worthy men—

Coquette.   And then I might have had 'em.

I now muſt marry what I can ;

Looking-Glass.   That's what you muſt, good Madam.

    - You ſee you can no longer paſs

    But for an aged crone ;

Coquette. To reſignation forc'd at laſt,

    I, Catharine, change my tone.

And ſo ſhe did indeed, poor Kate

    Now quite ſubdu'd, and civil,

Was marry'd, and, becauſe 'twas late,

    Contented with—a Devil.

T H E

Jc ne ſçais quel défin le lui diſoit auſſi :

Le Défin peut loger chez une piécieuſe

Celle-ci fit un choix qu'on n'auroit jamais crû,

Se trouvant à la fin tout aiſe & tout heureuſe

    De rencontrer un Malôtru.

The WOLF and the LAMB.

AN old Ewe once had twins, and th'affectionate Mother
 At a distance was suckling the Daughter,
Whilst her other unlucky, but favourite Lamb,
 Was quenching his thirst in the water.

The Wolf, a lean, infamous, hungry sinner,
 Coming up, and approaching the brink,
Without doubt intended the Lamb for his dinner,
 Yet only pretended to drink.

At

Le Loup & l'Agneau.

UN Agneau se désaltéroit
 Dans le courant d'une onde pure;
Un Loup survient à jeun, qui cherchoit aventure,
 Et que la faim en ces lieux attiroit.

Qu

At firſt he roar'd out, in a violent rage,

    (In excuſe for his murderous ſcheme)

Declaring no creatures their thirſt could aſſuage,

    Whilſt he wantonly troubled the ſtream.

Be not angry, Sir, I mean no diſreſpect;

    Yet cannot help wiſhing, that Kings,

As well as their Subjects, would ſometimes reflect,

    And examine the nature of things.

The rivulet's clear gliding current runs South,

    And I cannot in any degree

Diſturb the ſtream; which muſt meet with your Ma-

    jeſty's mouth

    Long before it can ever reach me.

                      You

Qui te rend ſi hardi de troubler mon breuvage?

    Dit cet Animal, plein de rage.

Tu feras châtié de la témérité.

Sire, répond l'Agneau, que vôtre Majeſté

    Ne ſe mette pas en colere,

    Mais plûtôt qu'elle conſidere

    Que je me vas déſaltérant

        Dans le courant,

    Plus de vingt pas au-deſſous d'elle;

                    Et

You little impudent fcoundrel—fuch logical reafon
    Unpunifh'd, no Sovereign hears;
To remonftrate with Majefty thus—'tis high treafon,
    And I'll ftrip your fkin over your ears:

Laft fummer, befides, bleating one at another,
    Your fcandalous vile tittle-tattle
Was all about me; though, good Madam, your mother
    Pretended 'twas innocent prattle:

I was loaded with curfes, my coufin averr'd,
    Who, by *chance*, was not far from the fold;
And by whom, all your vile converfation was heard,
    And ev'ry fyllable faithfully told.

With

Et que, par confequent, en aucune façon,
    Je ne puis troubler fa boiffon.
Tu la troubles, reprit cette Bête cruelle;
Et je fçai que de moi tu médis l'an paffé.
Comment l'aurois-je fait fi je n'etois pas né?
    Reprit l'Agneau, je tâte encore de ma mère.

With reproach, Sir, to mention your name, I should

    scorn ;

  Me your Majesty takes for another ;

Since I've made it appear 'twas before I was born,

  Why then, Mr. Pert, 'twas your brother.

I've no brother ; your Majesty certainly dreams ;

  Then 'twas some of your infamous clan ;

Dogs and Shepherds were planning their infamous

    schemes,

  The poor innocent Wolf to trepan.

What beast could this tyrant in villainy match ?

  A Dogmatical impudent sinner !

Who, creating himself Jury, Judge, and Jack Ketch,

  Executed the Lamb for his dinner.

                    THE

    Si ce n'est toi, c'est donc ton frere.

Je n'en ai point. C'est donc quelqu'un des tiens ;

    Car vous ne m'epargnez guère,

    Vous, vos Bergers, et vos Chiens.

On me l'a dit, il faut que je me venge.

    Là-dessus, au fond des forêts,

    Le Loup l'emporte, et puis le mange,

    Sans autre forme de procès.

                    Le

The EAGLE and the OWL.

TO make up their quarrels, which long had subsisted,
    An Owl and an Eagle agreed .
That each other their children should spare, 'twas insisted,
    And without altercation decreed.

Whilst the new royal Friends were embracing each other,
    And their Subjects were singing Tē Deum,
My children, says Madge (an affectionate mother)
    Does your Majesty know when you see 'em ?

N

L'Aigle et le Hibou.

L'AIGLE et le Chat-huant leurs querelles cessèrent,
    Et firent tant qu'ils s'embrassèrent.
L'un jura foi de Roi, l'autre foi de Hibou,
Qu'ils ne se goberoient leurs petits peu ni prou.   •
Connoissez-vous les miens ? dit l'Oiseau de Minerve.

N

5

No indeed, fays the Monarch ;—in forrowful tone
    The fond mother expreffes her fears,
Then whenever you find them, 'tis fifty to one
    But their fkins are ftrip'd over their ears :

Gods and Kings, when incontinent, forfeit their word
    For their appetite's fake ; and inveigle
Their credulous fubjects, fays Pallas's bird,
    But I'll truft neither Jove nor his Eagle.

Says the Monarch, be patient, I've not often blafted
    Your family's hopes, my dear Madam :
The flefh of your Children I fcarce ever tafted ;
    At our table we feldom have had 'em.

                              But

Non, dit l'Aigle. Tant pis, reprit le trifte Oifeau,
    Je crains, en ce cas, pour leur peau.
    C'eft hazard, fi je les conferve.
Comme vous êtes Roi, vous ne confidérez
Qui ni quoi . Rois et Dieux mettent, quoiqu'on leur die,
    Tout en même Catégorie.
Adieu mes nourriffons, fi vous les rencontrez.

        G   Peignet.

But to me, for the future, whilst searching for food,
    Should chance accidentally shew 'em;
Since I've sworn to destroy not the delicate brood,
    Pray describe them, and then I shall know 'em;

And shall treat most respectfully, Madam, your race,
    When I meet with your Highness's nest;
With absolute caution avoiding the place
    Where the dear little *Ganymedes rest*:

With professional friendship and flattery smooth'd,
    His Majesty's speech was believ'd:
When fond Mothers, alas! are by vanity sooth'd,
    Then are Pallas's Daughters deceiv'd.

To

Peignez-les moi, dit l'Aigle, ou bien me les montrez,
    Je n'y toucherai de ma vie.

To defcribe her dear Children the Mother begins——
    I without partiality fwear,
When my Darlings are hatch'd (for I always have twins)
    You'll not find a more Beautiful Pair.

From their fhape (by Dame Nature fo well are they made)
    You may trace out *the Beautiful Line,*
Which might *Bunbury*'s accurate pencil perfuade
    To copy the partial defign :

But outlines are enough, your fagacity now,
    Sir, will eafily guefs at the reft,
And my young ones from others undoubtedly know,
    When your Majefty meets with my neft.

                          Having

Le Hibou repartit · Mes petits fon mignons,
Beaux, bien faits, & jolis, fui tous leurs compagnons :
Vous les reconnoîtrez fans peine à cette marque.
N'allez pas l'oublier : retenez-la fi bien
    Que chez moi la maudite Parque
    N'entre point par votre moyen.

Having modeftly waited till twilight, fhe trudges,
 Any longer impatient to tarry;
And, meeting with *one of his Majefty's Judges*,
 Perfuaded his Lordfhip to marry.

No quibbling delays could the nuptials impede,
 As the Bridegroom belong'd to the law;
The Prieft pray'd that the new-married couple might breed,
 And the Lady was foon in the ftraw:

Little Judges were hatch'd—but before they were flown,
 What by chance fhould Jove's minifter fee,
But two tender young Devils, all cover'd with down,
 Peeping out of an old hollow tree?

'Mongft

Il avint qu'au Hibou Dieu donna géniture.
De façon qu'un beau foir qu'il étoit en pâture,
 Notre Aigle apperçut d'avanture,
 Dans les coins d'une roche dure,
 Où dans les trous d'une mazure,
 (Je ne fçai pas lequel des deux)
 De petits Monftres fort hideux,

Rechigné,

'Mongſt five hundred and fifty ridiculous ſights,
        You never could ſee ſuch another;
Of countenance woeful, diminutive Knights,
        They both ſeem'd afraid of each other;

One was grinning, and rolling his black marble eyes,
        T'other ſnapping his petulant bill;
Though prodigious at firſt was the Monarch's ſurprize,
        He determin'd his belly to fill.

Theſe are nothing like Owls—I may ſafely proceed,
        And the ſhrill ſhrieking Devils ſhall ſeize:
By the Mother's deſcription, Madge never could breed
        Such horrible monſters as theſe.

                                        She

Rechignés, un air triſte, une voix de Mégére,
    Ces enfans ne ſont pas, dit l'Aigle, à notre ami :
    Croquons-les. Le galand n'en fit pas a demi.
    Ses repas ne ſont point repas à la légère.

                    G 2   L'Hibou,

She was abfent, in fearch of provifions to roam,

And returning from market with meat ;

Inftead of her dear little Darlings at home,

She nothing could find but their feet.

The Moufe, whilft poor Madge was like Niobe fhrieking,

Vain provifion !-jump'd out of her jaws ;

And the glad little Chicken efcap'd, which was fqueaking,

No longer retentive her claws.

She call'd upon Pallas, and Jupiter too,

To punifh the murderous finner ;

But what could the Gods or the Goddeffes do,

When their Eagle had had his dinner.

That

L'Hibou, de retour, ne trouve que les piéds

De fes chers nourifſons, helas ! pour toute chofe.

Il fe plaint ; & les Dieux fon par lui fuppliés

De punir le brigand qui de fon deuil eft caufe.

Quelqu'un lui dit alors : n'en accufe que toi,

Ou plûtôt la commune loi,

Qui

That the Mother's imprudence and vanity flew

    Both her Children, at laft 'twas infifted;

For partially guiding the pencil, fhe drew

    The refemblance which never exifted.

                         T H E

    Qui veut qu'on trouye fon femblable

    Beau, bien fait, & fur tous aimable.

Tu fis de tes enfans à l'Aigle ce portrait :

    En avoient-ils le moindre trait?

The LION, the WOLF, and the FOX.

AN old Lion, with age
   More decrepid, than fage,
Was determin'd to grow young again ;
To tell obftinate Kings
Of impoffible things,
Without doubt is to labour in vain.

That

Le Lion, le Loup, & le Renard.

UN Lion décrépit, gouteux, n'en pouvant plus
   Vouloit que l'on trouvât remède à la vieilleffe;
Alleguer l'impoffible aux Rois, c'eft un abus.

Celui-

That all might attend

Their affiftance to lend,

He fent for the Medical Pack:

And faid, fome fhould prefcribe

Out of every tribe,

The Phyfician as well as the Quack.

From various parts,

Skill'd in phyfical arts,

What coxcomical numbers appear?

Cats, Monkies, and Pigs,

Drefs'd in full-bottom'd wigs,

But, alas! Dr. Fox was not there.

The

Celui-ci, parmi chaque efpèce,

Manda des Médecins: il en eft de tous arts:

Médecins au Lion viennent de toutes parts:

De tous côtés lui vient des donneurs de recettes.

'Dans les vifites qui font faites,

Le Renard fe difpenfe, & fe tient clos & coi.

Le

The Wolf, approaching the bed,

Like a fycophant, faid,

Shall the Fox then his vifits poftpone?

The Doctor's at home,

And, not caring to come,

Muft intend an affront to the Throne:

On this grand confultation

The good of the nation

Depends —— Says the King, in a wrath,

With fire and fmoke

The vile rafcal we'll choke,

If he does not crawl out of his earth,

And

Le Loup en fait fa cour, daube au concher du Roi,
Son camarade abfent, le Prince tout-à-l'heure
Veut qu'on aille enfumer Renard dans fa demeure,

Qu'on

And directly appear —

But, fays Reynard, I'm here;

For the fly cunning cur had found out,

By fome one who went,

Or intelligence fent,

Of what Dr. Wolf was about.

To conceive 'twas neglect,

Or, what's worfe, difiefpect,

Your Majefty, Sir, is too wife:

To fpeak plain, and be bold,

You've been certainly told

A parcel of infamous lyes:

I to

Qu'on le faffe venir. Il vient, eft préfenté;

Et fachant que le Loup lui faifoit cette affaire.

Je crains, Sire, dit-il, qu'un rapport peu fincére

Ne m'ait à mépris imputé

D'avoir différé cet hommage :

Mais

I to offer up vows

For your health (Heaven knows!)

A perilous Pilgrimage made;

Or, believe me, no one

At the foot of the Throne

With more pleafure his homage had paid.

To Phyficians of learning,

And men of difcerning,

Whilft I travel'd, your cafe was related:

That the whole Commonwealth

On your Majefty's health

Was depending, I faithfully ftated.

Ev'ry

Mais j'étois en pélérinage,

Et m'acquittois d'un vœu fait pour votre fanté.

Même j'ai vû dans mon voyage

Gens experts & favans, leur ai dit la langueur

Dont votre Majefté craint à bon droit la fuite:

Vous

Ev'ry one of them faid,

(Whilft fhaking his head,)

That the natural warmth was deftroy'd;

That in every vein

You would vigour regain,

If frefh animal warmth was employ'd:

The fecret is this

(And indeed not amifs,

Prefcribing what's eafily got)

That no med'cine can more

Feeble nature reftore,

Than——the fkin of a Wolf fmoking hot.

When

Vous ne manquez que de chaleur :
Le long âge en vous l'a détruite.
D'un Loup écorché vif appliquez-vous la peau
Tout chaude & toute fumante ·
Le fecret, fans doute, en eft beau
Pour la nature défaillante.

Meffire

When th experiment's try'd,

Let th' event but decide,

If your Majesty pleases, we'll do't:

And now, to proceed,

Dr. Wolf must be flay'd,

And shall furnish the *Royal Surtout*.

Not hearing his pray'rs,

Nor regarding his tears,

To strip him Physicians begin;

With part of his flesh

They their Monarch refresh,

And envelop him warm in the skin.

THE

Messire Loup vous servira,

S'il vous plaît, de robe-de-chambre.

Le Roi goûte cet avis-là?

On écorche, on taille, on démembre

Messire Loup. Le Monarque en soupa,

Et de sa peau s'enveloppa.

Le

The ENGLISH FOX.

ADDRESSED TO THE PEOPLE OF ENGLAND.

YOU'RE noble-minded, free, liberal, friendly, sedate;
    And have talents to govern the nation:
Had I twice fifty tongues I could never relate
    All your excellent qualifications.

Those Elements (lately which Englishmen brav'd
    In the glorious month of September *)
From the jaws of destruction your enemies sav'd,
    Must with gratitude ever remember.

* 13th of Sept. 1782, Floating Batteries destroyed before Gibraltar.

To

Le Renard Anglois.

LE bon cœur est chez vous compagnon du bon sens,
    Avec cent qualités trop longues à déduire,
Un noblesse d'âme, un talent pour conduire
        Et les affaires & les gens;
Un humeur franche & libre, & le don d'être amie,
Malgré Jupiter même, & les temps orageux.
Tout cela méritoit un éloge pompeux:
Il en eût été moins, selon votre génie.

La

I

To all other countries your own is preferr'd;
   A true Briton dislikes an Exotic:
And, though the maxim, perhaps, is condemn'd as absurd,
   He thinks he cannot be too patriotic.

By climate assisted, your temperate minds
   Are all given to deep meditation;
Your improvements in science the Foreigner finds,
   And they meet with his just approbation.

To prove ingenuity never is idle,
   We'll examine your riding attire:
An Englishman's saddle, boots, breeches, and bridle,
   With envy French Jockies admire:

                                 They'll

La pompe vous déplaît, l'éloge vous ennuie:
J'ai donc fait celui-ci court & simple. Je veux
    Y coudre encore un mot ou deux
    En faveur de votre patrie:
Vous l'aimez. Les Anglois pensent profondément;
Leur esprit en cela suit leur tempérament.
Creusant dans les sujets, & forts d'expériences,
Ils étendent par-tout l'empire des Sciences.
Je ne dis point ceci pour vous faire ma cour.

They'll attend when the Killer of Vermin begins
    To mention his Dogs and his Doxies;
But, delighted, will almost jump out of their skins,
    When he talks of your excellent Foxes;

To prove that they're wiser, and others excel,
    A miraculous tale I'll unfold;
The common tricks of a Fox any body can tell,
    But my tale never yet has been told:

A notorious Fox, press'd exceedingly hard
    By a numerous pack in full cry,
Accidentally ran through a Game-keeper's yard,
    Where the Traitor was ready to die:

                          At

Vos gens, à penetrer, l'emportent sur les autres:
    Même les Chiens de leur séjour
    Ont meilleur nez que n'ont les nôtres.
Vos Renards sont plus fins, je m'en vais le prouver
    Par un d'eux, qui, pour se sauver,
    Mit en usage un stratagême
Non encor pratiqué, des mieux imaginés.
Le scélérat réduit en un péril extrême,
Et presque mis à bout par ces Chiens au bon nez

                        Passa

At one end of the barn, *in terrorem* fufpended,

    The Villain could inftantly fee

Many thieves, who their lives in difgrace had thus ended,

    Malefactors of ev'ry degree ;

Brother Foxes, ftate Traitors, vile Badgers, and Cats,

    Were all honour'd with feparate pegs ;

Whilft Hawks, Kites, and Magpies, Spread Eagles, and

        Rats,

    Ev'ry one were nail'd up by the legs :

The poor Devil, exhaufted, yet able to crawl,

    Up amongft the good company fteals,

Where he found an unoccupied peg in the wall,

    And hung himfelf up by the heels :

                                 By

Paffa pres d'un patibulaire.

    Là, des Animaux raviffans,

Blereaux, Renards, Hiboux, race incline à mal faire,

Pour l'exemple pendus inftruiffoient les paffans.

Leur confrere, aux abois, entre ces morts s'arrange.

I

By neceffity thus reconcil'd and prepar'd,

    'Twas in confcience a wife *Coalition*;

Though arrang'd amongft thofe who, he'd often declar'd,

    Were with equity doom'd to perdition :

None but Hannibal thus could prevent an affault,

    Ev'ry perfon of judgment fuppofes ;

For he made his efcape, when the Romans, at fault,

    Were all puzzled, and cock'd up their nofes.

The leading Dogs arriv'd firft at the Game-keeper's door,

    Who feldom their Huntfman mifled,

He was clofe at their heels, and, faft galloping, fwore,

    That the Fox was ran under the bed ;

                        Determin'd

Je crois voir Annibal, qui preffe des Romains,

Met leurs Chefs en défaut, ou leur donne le change ;

Et fçut eu vieux Renard s'echapper de leurs mains.

    Les Clefs de meute parvenues

A l endroit ou pour mort le traître fe pendit,

          Remplirent

Determin'd that Reynard fhould forfeit his life,
 And kneeling down with her broom-ftick to kill—
Why there's no fuch a thing, fays the Game-keeper's wife;
 Look under the bed, if you will,

By this time came up all the reft of the chace
 In full cry—but their triumph was ended;
In a moment the fcent was thrown up at the place
 Where the fly cunning Cur was fufpended:

Whilft the Dogs in diftraction were rending the fkies,
 We depend on your nofes, fays *Meynel,*
Who declar'd that the Fox, whom they faw with their eyes,
 Some-where elfe was earth'd up in his kennel.

He

Remplirent l'air de cris: leur Maître les rompit,
Bien que de leurs abois ils percaffant les nues.
Il ne put foupçonner ce tour affez plaifant.
Quelque Terrier, dit-dil, a fauvé mon galant.

Mes

He commanded his Huntfman to call off the pack ;

    With reluctance his voice they regard,

Who inftantly leading them off, with a crack

    Trotted out of the Game-keeper's yard.

The Fox was hunted again; but not changing his rout,

    In his ftratagem ftill perfeveres ;

When the people as well as the pack found him out,

    And his fkin was ftript over his ears.

THE MORAL.

Whilft Englifhmen truft *Parliamentary Proxies*,

    If they be not infenfible logs,

They will let felf-fufpended political Foxes

    Defervedly go to the Dogs.

                             THE

    Mes Chiens n'appellent point au-delà des colonnes

        Où font tant d'honnêtes perfonnes.

   Il y viendra, le drôle. Il y vint, à fon dam.

      Voila maint Baffet clabaudant ;

   Voilà notre Renard, au charnier fe guindant ;

   Maître pendu croyoit qu'il en iroit de même

   Que le jour qu'il tendit de femblables panneaux :

   Mais le pauvret, ce coup, y laiffa fes houfeaux ·

   Tant il eft vrai qu'il faut changer de ftratagême.

             H 3   *Le*

The YOUNG COCK and the FOX,

YOUNG Chanticleer, perch'd on the branch of a
  tree,
 Was ftanding fentinel over his Pullet ;
And by chance, looking down at the bottom, could fee
 One—who thought of diftending his gullet;

A fly flatt'ring Fox, whofe foft eloquent voice
 Was addreffing the Pullet—to tell her,
" That whatever farm-yard had afforded the choice,
 " She'd pick'd out a fine beautiful fellow :

        " His

Le jeune Coq & le Renard.

SUR la branche d'un arbre étoit en fentinelle
  Un jeune Coq adroit, et matois.

         Frère,

" His dulciloquent voice is our conftant delight,

    " And ev'ry one of the neighbourhood know

" How often our *Houfe* keeps awake all the night,

    " When it hears the Young Gentleman crow."

Having talk'd to the Pullet in vain — whofe invention

    Seldom fails him, the Killer of Geefe

Next addreffes the Cock,—with beginning to mention

    The terms of a general peace.

" We're to quarrel no more," fays the fly cunning Devil,

    " But with joy muft each other embrace ;

" Vouchfafe, Sir, to put us but both on a level,

    " By coming down, and refigning your place :

                      " Don't

Frère, dit un Renaid, adouciffante fa voix,

    Nous ne fommes plus en querelle .

    Paix générale cette fois.

Je viens te l'annoncer , defcens, que je t'embraffe.

" Don't detain me, dear Sir ; I'm oblig'd to proceed,

" And deliver out many a letter,

" Containing glad tidings of peace to your breed ;

" The fooner you come down, the better.

" 'Gain't our fly cunning tricks now no longer you need

" All your dear brother Chickens forewarn ;

" Ev'ry one may be fafe, and in bus'nefs proceed,

" Whilft he pecks in the Treafury-barn.

" If you do not defcend, I fhall bleed at the heart,

" All your fcrupulous fears, Sir, difmifs ;

" I fhall die with diftraction, before I depart

" If I get not a brotherly kifs.

" If

Ne me retarde point de grace :

Je dois faire aujourd'hui vingt poftes fans manquei,

Les tiens & toi pouvez vaquer,

Sans nulle crainte, à vos affaires

Nous vous y fervirons en freres.

Faites-en les feux, dès ce foir,

Et cependant vient recevoir

Le baifer d'amour fraternelle.

A' h

" If for fashion's fake only, come down, my dear Brother,

    " And condefcend—for, whenever they meet,

" All our Gentlemen now kifs and hug one another,

    " Though 'tis in the midft of the ftreet "

Notwithftanding this flattering fpeech—in good truth

    The Young Cock was exceedingly ftaunch :

And at laft, like a prudent and eloquent Youth,

    Stepping forward, ftill ftood on the branch :

" To hear, Sir, that henceforward our quarrels fhall ceafe,

    " Affords me moft exquifite pleafure ;

" And with you, Sir, at leaft, always wifhing for peace,

    " I cannot but approve of the meafure,

                        " Which

Ami, reprit le Coq, je ne pouvois jamais

Apprendre une plus douce & meilleure nouvelle,

        Que celle

        De cette paix.

    Et ce m'eft une double joie

De la tenir de toi. Je vois deux Lévriers,

     Qui m'affure, font couriers,

     Que pour ce fujet on envoie.

" Which I doubted at firſt, and ſuppos'd 'twas a ſly

    " Cunning tale, which was told to decoy ;

" But two Meſſengers more I perceive, in full cry,

    " To bring the glad tidings of joy ;

" *Snap* and *Holdfaſt*, I mean ; they'll ſoon finiſh their chace,

    " Moſt joyfully joining our crew ;

" Then deſcending, we will with great pleaſure embrace

    " All together."—Says Reynard, " Adieu !

" You know, my dear Sir, that, in infinite haſte,

    " I've no time for ſuch long interviews ;

" And, becauſe I muſt travel exceedingly faſt,

    " Another time we'll talk over the news."

And

Ils vont vîte, & ſeront dans un moment à nous.

Je deſcens   nous pourrons nous entrebaiſer tous.

Adieu ! dit Renard, ma traite eſt longue à faire.

Nous nous réjouirons du ſuccès de l'affaire

    Un autre fois.   Le Galant auſſi-tôt

    Tire ſes g'égues, gagne au haut,

Mal-

And away the fly flattering Cur (with his fwitch

   'Tween his legs) moft difgracefully fteals,

As much frighten'd, as if the two Sons of a Bitch,

   Open-mouth'd, had been clofe at his heels.

DEATH

    Mal-content de fon ftratagême ;

    Et notre jeune Coq, en foi-même,

    Se mit à iire de fa peur :

Car c'eft double plaifir de tromper le trompeur.

La

DEATH AND THE DYING MAN.

Debilem facito manu,
Debilem pede coxâ :
Tuber adstrue gibberum,
Lubricos quate dentes,
Vita dum superest, benè est.
Hanc mihi, vel acutâ
Si sedeam cruce, sustine.

Vide SENEC. Epist. 101,

A Dying old Man, not forgetting his Heirs,
   Yet reluctantly taking his leave,
Poor Mortal! most ardently pleads his affairs,
   And impatiently begs a reprieve ;

Appall'd

La Mort & le Mourant.

UN Mourant, qui comptoit plus de cent ans de vie,
   Se plaignoit à la Morte, que précipitamment

Elle

Appall'd at the fight of his terrible dart—
   O Death! do not fuddenly kill,
And oblige a poor innocent Man to depart
   Without having finifh'd his will.

My Wife has declar'd that fhe means to partake
   Of my fate; and (can any one doubt her)
Prepar'd not at prefent the journey to take,
   Won't permit me to travel without her;

I've recently got a Great-grandfon, for whom
   To provide not would prove a difafter,
I've been building a Room, and not finifh'd the Dome,
   Having waited for Adams's plaifter.

                             Dame

Elle le contraignoit de partir tout à l'heure,
    Sans qu'il eût fait fon teflament,
Sans l avertir au moins   Eft-il jufte qu'on meure
Au p éd levé ? dit-il; attendez quelque peu
Ma Femme ne veut pas que je puite fans elle.
Il me refte à pourvoir un Arrière-neveu
Souffiez qu à mon logis j'aujoûte encore une aîle.

                             Que

Dame Proferpine's fummons I'd not difregard,
    If I was not confin'd by the gout :
I return many thanks for her Ladyfhip's card,
    But I cannot make one at her route.

Indignant Death—in different ftyle,
    (No longer to poftpone)
Grinn'd horrible—a ghaftly fmile,
    And made him change his tone.

'Tis fhameful fuch a Sage as you
    Should talk of Children's rattles,
Whilft Death hath fomething elfe to do,
    Than think of goods and chattels.

'Tis

Que vous êtes preffante. O Déeffe cruelle !
Vieil'ard, lui dit la Mort, je ne t'ai point furpris.
Tu te plains fans raifon de mon impatience
Eh n'as-tu pas cent ans ? Trouve moi dans Paris
Deux Mortels auffi vieux , trouve m'en dix en France.

Je

'Tis fhameful too, that fuch a Sage
    Should anxioufly complain ;
You're ninety-nine,—and that's an age,
    Few feldom can attain.

Ten thoufand younger men than you,
    Regardlefs of my dart,
In battle bid the world adieu,
    And willingly depart

* Thy tottering fteps, 'tis evident,
    To labour ftill conftrain'd,
Try to fupport a *Tenement*
    Which cannot be fuftain'd ;

                       Nor

---

* Ecclefiaftes, Chap vii — Vide Amœnitates Academicæ Linnæi,
vol. v.—Solomon on Old Age explained

    Je devois, ce dis tu, te donner quelque avis,
        Qui te difpofât à la chofe
    J'aurois trouvé ton teftament tout fait
    Ton petit-fils pourvû, ton bâtiment parfait,
    Ne te donna-t-on pas des avis, quand la caufe
        Du marcher & du mouvement

                       Quand

Nor can it ever be reftor'd,
 As various figns betoken,
For *loofen'd is the filver chord,*
 The golden bowl is broken :

Whilft all your faculties decreafe,
 Your nerves have loft their tone,
Becaufe they're few, the grinders ceafe ;
 Your appetite is gone.

Sweet Mufic's daughters now rejoice
 No longer—* though the viol
Awakes—to Melancholy's plaintive voice,
 Or Joy's extatic trial.

But

---

* See Collins's Ode for Mufic—The Paffions.

Quand les efprits, le fentiment,
Quand tout faillit en toi ? Plus de goût, p'us d'ouïe,
Toute chofe pour toi femble être évanouie ·
Pour toi l'aftre du jour prend des foins fuperflus :

Tu

But to be brief—I muſt attend
    This moment many a bed;
Remember, Sir, your every friend
    Is dying, if not dead.

You ſhall not then be left alone;
    Expect no ſecond warning:
The world, old Gentleman, will find you gone
    Before to-morrow morning.

T H E

Tu regrettes des biens qui ne te touchent plus.
    Je t'ai fait voir les Camaardes,
    Ou morts, ou mourans, ou malades.
Qu'eſt-ce que tout cela, qu'un avertiſſement ?
    Allons, Vieillard, & ſans réplique:
    Il n'importe à la République
    Que tu faſſes ton teſtament.

I

The GRASSHOPPER and the ANTS.

A Grafshopper, at home by cold winter confin'd,
  Survey'd her treafury-chamber in vain,
For not a grain our improvident Songfter could find,
  Her languifhing life to fuftain :

In fummer-time finging, more merry than wife,
  Happy creature ! fhe wanted no meat ;
In her interludes catching diminutive Flies,
  Ev'ry moment fhe met with a treat.

So

Le Cigale & la Fourmi.

L A Cigale ayant chanté
  Tout l'E'té,
Se trouva fort depourvûe
Quand la bife fut venue.
Pas un feul petit morceau
De Mouche ou de Vermiffeau.

Elle

So the warbling Syren, whenever she pleafes,

    From the fcenes of our Opera fhop

(With her mufic betwitching him) eafily feizes

    (Poor victim!) the fluttering Fop.

In full feather and fong she can thoufands engage,

    But she cannot catch amorous Beaux,

In the cruel penurious winter of age,

    When the ftorm of Adverfity blows.

To return—the poor Grafshopper, famifh'd, applies

    To a neighb'ring republic of Ants;

And, to move their compaffion her eloquence tries,

    In all humility telling her wants:

                               If

    Elle alla crier famine

    Chez la Fourmi fa voifine,

    La priant de lui prêter

    Quelque grain pour fubfifter

    Jufqu'a la faifon nouvelle.

    Je vous pairai, lui dit-elle,

    Avant l'Oût, foi d'animal,

    Intérêt & principal.

If you lend but a little, my life to fuſtain,
　　To return it indeed I'll remember,
And be gratefully thankful; and every grain
　　Will with intereſt pay in September:

But not one of Dame Induſtry's tribe would befriend her,
　　Hard queſtions, moreover, they aſk;
And (cruel Moraliſts!) now 'tis too late, reprehend her
　　For laſt ſummer neglecting her taſk.

Night and day you ſpent merrily ſinging?—'tis true:
　　For futurity truſting to Chance?
With empty ſtomachs, in winter-time what can you do?
　　You cannot do better than dance.

T H E

La Fourmi n'eſt pas prêteuſe:
C eſt là ſon moindre défaut.
Que faiſiez-vous au temps chaud?
Dit-elle à cette emprunteuſe.
Nuit & jour, à tout venant
Je chantois, ne vous deplaiſe.
Vous chantiez? J'en ſuis fort aiſe:
Hé bien, danſez maintenant.

5

L'Alouette

The LARK and her YOUNG ONES, with the MASTER of the FIELD.

WHEN Feather'd Folks are all pairing themselves
       two and two,

And Dame Nature is making a *hullibaloo*,

The Turkey Cock gobbles, and Quack ! goes the Drake,

Diving merrily after his Duck in the lake.

Frighten'd out of the church by the Parson and People,

Noisy Jackdaws are choosing their wives in the steeple;

As devoutly employ'd as the Preacher (we prove)

For what is the warmest devotion, but love ?

When the wise little Architect, artless, the Wren,

Tells his amorous tale to the dear little Hen ;

When the nimble Tom-tit rounds the tree, to discover

The snug little hole, for himself and his Lover;

You

L'Alouette & ses Petits, avec le Maître d'un Champ.

LES Alouettes font leur nid
    Dans les bléds quand ils font en herbe ;
C'est-à-dire, environ le temps
Que tout aime, & que tout pollule dans la monde :
   Monstres marins au fond de l'onde,
Tigres dans les forêts, Alouettes aux champs.

Un

You will poffibly think a poor Fabulift crazy,

For ever believing a Lark could be lazy :

Yet 'tis true ; for more modeft, perhaps, than the reft,

There was certainly one, who, forgetting her neft,

Like an unfettled Mortal (for ever on wing)

Had undoubtedly loft the beft part of the fpring :

At laft, prompted by Nature, as well as another,

She determin'd, tho' late, to commence the fond Mother;

And fhe flies to *Dame Ceres*, and earneftly begs,

In the midft of the corn to depofit her eggs ;

Where, inftinctively fix'd, with affectionate pleafure,

For a time the fond Mother broods over her treafure ,

Whilft humble, yet lofty, whilft warbling, devout,

Is the Cock's early note, when Aurora fets out ;

For, leaving the ground, rifing upwards, He flies

On Gratitude's wings, mounting up to the fkies ;

In his fong are the praifes of Providence found,

For guarding his Hen in her neft on the ground .

But

Un portant de ces dernières,
Avoit laiffé paffer la moitié d'un printemps
Sans goûter les plaifirs des amours printannières.
A toute force enfin elle fe réfolut
D'imiter la Nature , & d'être Mère encore.

Elle

But thefe heavenly flights he no longer purfues,

When his favourite Partner has told him the news:

" You've now fomething better to do than to fing,

" As you'll find, if you will but peep under my wing ;

" In the midft of the clouds you can pick up no food,

" And empty bills, we both know, cannot nourifh our brood."[2]

Before the tale was well told, the dear diligent Fellow

Was flown again ; for he ftaid not a moment to tell her

With what affectionate care, and parental delight,

He fhould fearch for (by no perpendicular flight)

Amongft Nature's diminutive tribes, a repaft ;

Determin'd their clamorous brood fhould not faft.

Had I five thoufand tongues I could never relate

Half thofe infects the dear little *Dunftables* ate :

As their Parents were at it from morning till night,

What numberlefs victims were ftopt in their flight !

For

Elle bâtit un nid, pond, couve, & fait éclore,
A la hâte, le tout alla du mieux qu'il put.   1

For they feiz'd on fometimes (not regarding the fting)

But a bit of a Wafp, or a Butterfly's wing;

Grafshoppers lamented the lofs of their feet,

For almoft every creature they met with was meat.

And thefe Larks (from their Parents' protection releas'd)

Are to make a fide-difh at an Alderman's feaft:

But no matter for that, fince 'twill never be known

What becomes of their volatile brood, when 'tis flown:

Thofe Children whom they'll not recall,

But let the wanderers foar;

And then, rejoicing once for all,

They'll never know them more.

By Providence at firft employ'd,

Forgetting dear connections

In future time, they thus avoid

Ten thoufand keen reflections.

What

What confolation can affuage
 The Mothers of Mankind?
Whofe generous warlike Sons engage
 With elements combin'd:

And when their fate is too well known,
 (Their winding-fheet a wave,)
Grey hairs at home *are then brought down*
 With forrow to the grave.

To return to the Larks—though we find 'em not flown,
And imperfectly fledg'd, they're amazingly grown;
And with exquifite pleafure the Mother defcries
That they've cock'd up their bills, and have open'd their eyes.
But now, changing her colours, *Dame Ceres* was feen
In her *demi-faifon*, neither yellow nor green;
And 'fore the Mother could fee the dear favourites flown,
The *Goddefs* had put on her ftraw-colour'd gown.

        When

Les b'éds d'alentour mûrs, avant que la nitée
  Se trouvât affez forte encor
  Pour voler, & prendre l'effor,

        De

When the *provident Creature* began to reveal

Both her fears and her cautious advice—*en famille*;

Whilft peeping from under her wing, in their turns,

Every one his firft leffon attentively learns .—

" With his Servants and Sons, when the Farmer appears

" Ev'ry one muft immediately prick up his ears ;

" Our future conduct depending on what they fhall fay,

" Whether fooner or later to fcamper away —

" A fingle fyllable muft not from me be conceal'd."

She was flown, when the Farmer appear'd in the field,

And examin'd an ear, which he rubb'd in his hand :—

" This corn is quite ripe, and no longer fhall ftand;

" Give

De mille foins divers l'Alouette agitée,

S'en va chercher pâture, avertit fes enfans

D'être toujours au guet, & faire fentinelle.

Si le Poffeffeur de ces Champs

Vient avec fon Fils, comme il viendra, dit-elle,

Ecoutez bien : felon ce qu'il dira,

Chacun de nous décampera.

Si-tôt que l'Alouette eût quitté fa famille,

Le Poffeffeur du Champ vient avec fon Fils.

Ces

" Give all my friends warning

" To meet in the morning;

" Let ev'ry one come with his fickle."

The Larks, from their fright,

Were in horrible plight,

And their neft in a terrible pickle.

Soon the Mother return'd with a mouthful of meat,

Which none of her vigilant Watchmen would eat;

And whilft fhe was wondering what was the matter,

Every one at a time were beginning to chatter;

But the Cock of the neft,

More aleit than the reft,

And a favourite Bird of his Mother's,

Was appointed the Speaker,

And, 'caufe they were weaker,

Boldly perch'd on the backs of his Brothers:

" Again

Ces bléds font mûrs, dit-il   Allez chez nos amis,

Les prier que chacun apportant fa faucille,

Nous vienne a der demain dès la pointe du jour.

Notre Alouette de retour

Tiouve en alarme fa couvée.

L'un

" Again the Farmer was here—

" If the morning is clear,

" All his friends will be with him by five :

" Slashing work will be made,

" They'll cut down ev'ry blade,

" And such a havoc we cannot survive."

" A fine maiden speech !

" But I beg and beseech

" You'd no more put yourselves in a pother ;

" Since the bus'nefs depends

" On the help of those friends,

" Who'll none of them come," says the Mother.

She

L'un commence· Il a dit, que l'Aurore levée,

L'on fit venir demain fes amis, pour l'aider.

S il n'a dit que cela, repartit l'Alouette,

Rien ne nous preffe encor de changer de retraite

Mais c'eft demain qu'il faut tout de bon écouter.

Cependant foyez gais. voilà de quoi manger.

Eux repûs, tout s'endort, les Petits & la Mère.

L'aube

She was certainly right,

Though the morning was bright,

Yet the poor Farmer's friends were too fickle;

If the truth could be known,

They'd all crops of their own,

And at home were at work with the fickle.

Still the provident Lark

Bids her young ones remark,

And 'bove all the dear favourite Bird :

" To-morrow's the day,

" You muft mind what they fay,

" And remember to tell ev'ry word.

" Take

L'aube du jour arrive , & d'amis point du tout.

L'Alouette à l'effor, le Maître s'en vient faire

Sa ronde ainfi qu'à l'ordinaire :

Ces bléds ne devroient pas, dit-il, étre debout.

Nos amis ont grand tort, & toit qui fe repofe

Sur de tels pareffeux à fervir ainfi lents .

Mon Fils, allez chez nos parens

Les prier de la même chofe.

L'épouvante

" Take courage, I beg,

" (And this Butterfly's egg)

" To-night, at leaſt, in ſecurity reſt ."*

And expanding her wings

O'er the dear little things,

Moſt completely ſhe cover'd the neſt.

In the morning ſhe flew

Without bidding adieu,

Soon intending to bring them their meat;

She return'd—but, behold !

Such a ſtory was told,

That ſhe thought it high time to retreat:

For

L'épouvante eſt au nid plus forte que jamais.
Il a dit ſes parens : Mère, c'eſt à cette heure——
Non, mes enfans, dormez en paix :
Ne bougeons de notre demeure.
L'Alouette eût raiſon, car perſonne ne vint.

Pour

For the Farmer again

Came, without any men :—

" We'll wait no longer for friend or relation ;

" By myfelf and my Son

" Shall the work be begun,

" And our diligence make reparation

" (Without any coft)

" For the time which is loft ;

" And this moment we both will begin :

" We'll no longer repine ;

" Since the weather is fine

" We fhall certainly foon get it in."

Though

Pour la troifième fois le Maître fe fouvint
De vifiter fes bléds.   Notre erreur eft extrême,
Dit-il, de nous attendre à d'autres gens que nous.
Il n'eft meilleur ami ni parent que foi-même.
Retenez bien cela, mon Fils ; & favez-vous
Ce qu'il faut faire ? Il faut qu'avec notre famille,
Nous prenions dés demain chacun une faucille :
C'eft-là nôtre plus court, & nous achéverons
     Notre moiffon quand nous pourrons.

Dès-lors

Though not attacking by ſtorm,

That their taſk they'd perform

Very ſoon, the wiſe Mother computes;

And, though proper the meaſure,

Yet ſtill, at her leiſure,

Marches off with Aurora's Recruits.

Dès-lors que le deſſein fut ſû de l'Alouette,

C'eſt à ce coup qu'il faut décamper, mes enfans:

Et les Petits en même temps

Voletans, ſe culebutans,

Délogèrent tous ſans trompette.

F I N I S.

Lightning Source UK Ltd.
Milton Keynes UK
UKHW022259301120
374378UK00005B/735